MW01029042

See with New Eyes

TY GIBSON

Pacific Press® Publishing Association
Nampa, Idaho
Oshawa, Ontario, Canada
www.pacificpress.com

For Amber, Jason and Leah

What a privilege it is to be your father!
May the incomparable beauty of your heavenly
Father's character ever hold you in awe.

Graphic design by Matthew McVane
Cover art by Nathan Green

Copyright © 2000 by Pacific Press®Publishing Association
All rights reserved
Printed in the United States of America

Additional copies of this book may be purchased at
http://www.adventistbookcenter.com

All Scripture quotations are from the King James
Version unless otherwise noted. NKJV indicates the New
King James Version. NIV indicates the New International Version.
NASB indicates the New American Standard Bible.

All emphasis and words in brackets within
quotations are added by the author.

Some of the names and details in stories have been
changed to protect the privacy of the individuals involved.

Library of Congress Cataloging-in-Publication Data:

Gibson, Ty, 1963-
See with new eyes : the true beauty of God's character / Ty Gibson
p. cm.
ISBN: 0-8163-1786-0
1. God. 2. God—Worship and love. 3. Christian life—Seventh-day
Adventist authors. I. Title

BT102 .G53 2000
231—dc21   00-026841

CONTENTS

ONE   Meeting My Father 5

TWO   What Do You See? 15

THREE   Look Again...For the First Time 25

FOUR   How God Looks in the Dark 33

FIVE   How God Looks in the Mirror 41

SIX   The Awakening Kiss 49

SEVEN   Blind in the Light 57

EIGHT   Destiny: Consciousness 63

NINE   Love Beyond Knowledge 73

TEN   Life in Love 85

ELEVEN   Timeless Calvary 95

TWELVE   Sight for Sore Eyes 109

THIRTEEN   Your Reflection in His Eyes 119

FOURTEEN   The Lie That Blinds 129

FIFTEEN   Because We're Free, We Need to See 137

SIXTEEN   What You See Is What You Get 145

SEVENTEEN   Feel What You See 155

ONE
MEETING MY FATHER

Knowing the true character of God is the

in the knowledge of His goodness and love. We tap

ultimate liberation. All freedom is present

in by believing.

As a little boy there was a period of time when I took refuge in a tree. I survived there in its highest branches.

Each day I'd come home from school like all boys do. Pausing at the front door with a lingering sense of yesterday's nervousness, I would dump my books and lunch pail on the porch and head for the tree in the front yard. There were three boards I had strategically nailed to the trunk as hand and foot holds so I could reach the first branch. Gaining height with each successive maneuver upward, I felt better and better. I felt safe.

Near the top of the tree there were two strong branches that formed a comfortable cradle. There I would sit, sometimes for hours, just thinking. Actually, most of the time was spent feeling. Feeling thoughts I could hardly think. I didn't really know what to think. My thoughts were nearly shapeless. But my feelings were very defined, and very strong. They were feelings of anger. Feelings of hatred. Feelings of deep desire for things to be different than they were. . .in that house down there that was supposed to be a home. Somehow I felt okay in the tree, in a sense, even though it was the place where I faced my reality with the most acute pain. At least I was alone. At least I was separated from those sights and sounds which made life nearly unbearable.

But as all boys must eat and sleep and do homework, I always came down from the tree. Mother would call and I would reluctantly climb back to earth, take a deep breath and walk through that door.

Sometimes the atmosphere was cheerful. Most of the time it was not. My mom was always trying to be happy, and my dad was always trying to crush out any possibility of happiness. The mental pictures are still vivid, but I rarely browse through them.

We'd all be sitting around the dining room table eating dinner. Gradually, with each drink of Kessler's or Vodka, tension would build. Over little stuff. The way the food was prepared. Mom's use of time. The bills. Whatever. Sometimes he would retain composure through the meal and vent his rage later in the night. Sometimes he would begin to throw dishes off the table, or he'd just turn the whole table over. Finally, it always ended up the same way. Mom would be beaten, often times bloody, sometimes unconscious. We four children were never touched by his violence, but we felt it beneath our skin in our hearts. Many nights we huddled in one bed, crying until the exhaustion would force us to sleep.

Then came the day of liberation, at least for me, at least to some degree.

My grades were down. The teacher called Mom and explained that I seemed distracted and was barely even doing my schoolwork. Mrs. Saunders told her that I was a child of above average intelligence, which I was proud to hear, but that I would have to repeat the second grade if I didn't start engaging in the learning process.

Mom was worried about me.

What a wonderful lady she was! She was the only person in the world who could make me smile. If there was anything I knew at all, I knew my mom loved me. The reason I hated Dad so much was because I loved her so much. The pain he was causing her was more than I could bear. Often I wished he were not my father.

Mom called up into the tree one day, "Ty, please come down. I need to talk with you before Charlie gets home."

"That's strange," I thought, "she called him *Charlie*." Normally, when talking to us children, she called him *Dad*. There was an unusual urgency in her voice.

I quickly climbed down and ran into the house. Mom led me into the den at the rear of the house and shut the door. We were alone. She began by talking about my grades at school. Then she said something about the fact that since I was the oldest of the children, I might understand something she felt a need to tell me. Maybe it would relieve me, she suggested, so I could focus on my schoolwork. Or maybe I wouldn't understand and it would make things worse. She wasn't sure. "But I think I need to go ahead and tell you," she said.

I was perplexed.

"What is she talking about?" I wondered to myself.

She reached over and put her pretty, young hands on my knees and looked at me straight and clear in the eyes. I remember feeling like she was going to tell me something very important, something that would help.

And she did.

"Charlie is not your dad," her voice cracked with restrained emotion.

"What?" I blurted out.

He was all I knew. I had always called him *Dad.* I was confused.

Then Mom pulled something out of an envelope. It was a photo of another man. The face was not familiar to me.

"His name is Johnny," she said. "He is your dad."

She proceeded to tell me what a nice man he was. Funny. Kind. Never violent. But she also told me that they were too young when I came along. He couldn't seem to settle down from his teenage party life. So she reluctantly left him after repeated warnings and desperate pleas that she wanted to have a "good life." She wanted something better for her baby. . .*baby Ty.*

"Charlie is not your dad," she repeated. "I hope somehow it helps to know that, because I know you don't like the way he treats your mommy."

While I never really understood why it didn't work out with my real dad, a major change took place inside of me that day. Over and over again I said to myself, "He's not my dad." Somehow, on some level, I was free; free to not identify with his ugliness; free to be someone else, to be unlike him.

I never called Charlie *Dad* again. My grades at school came up. And I never climbed the tree again, except for fun, which is the reason kids ought to climb trees. But my childhood liberation was only a faint shadow of a greater freedom yet to come.

Finally, after nine years of hell on earth, Mom divorced Charlie and ventured out to try and raise four children on her own. Divorced and alone, she worked hard, from morning till night every day, with an occasional Sunday off. We hardly ever saw her, but we knew she was working for us. It was the only way to survive. What else could she do?

With lots of time on my hands, I gravitated to the streets of the big city through which I walked to and from school each day. I guess I saw too much on those streets. Too much injustice. Too much heartache. Too much suffering.

Drug addiction. Drug babies. Racial hatred. Gang violence. Child abuse. It was all there, and it was all too much. Life was terrifyingly ugly, more ugly than I could cope with. So I got cynical, because I could never get numb, although I tried. Somehow, against my will, I felt every tragedy I witnessed. *Why couldn't anyone do something to stop it all?* I often questioned in my head.

But who was I talking to, as though there was some hidden reality of goodness and justice out there somewhere?

God wasn't even an option. I hadn't really ever encountered the idea in any concrete form. There was a vague notion that there must be some Higher Being, but it was nothing more than vague. I had heard other people talk about such a Being. Just who or what He or it was, I really didn't have a clue. There was this "ridiculous idea" some people had that God was a person, of sorts, and that He was good, that He actually loved people.

"How could anyone believe such nonsense?" I would think in my young, groping mind. "What a colossal heap of irrational hype. Just look at this world. Duh! Any moron can see that if there is a God, He sure doesn't give a rip about what's going on down here."

A distinct sense of perplexity and dissatisfaction deepened as time passed.

Then I met my Father. Not Johnny, but Jehovah.

I was seventeen and restless. My mom had become a Christian, as "an emotional survival effort," I assumed. To make matters worse, my girlfriend was also getting into this *God thing* as she studied the Bible with my mom. But I was immovable. There was no way, I kept telling myself, that God could be the kind of person I would want anything to do with. Case closed! Period!

Actually it wasn't a period, but rather a question mark. Somewhere deep inside I really wanted to understand the truth behind this whole blurry mess of a world. But there was no way I could simply accept, with blind gullibility, that God loves people. I needed sensible, logical answers.

My mom asked a youth pastor to try and visit with me once a week during a group Bible study she was hosting at our house. They'd study in the dining room and he'd come knock on my bedroom door, where I was hiding until the church people would leave. The first time he came to my room I was blown away by the boldness of this suit-wearing, short-haired "geek" trying to interest me in religious matters. But his courage aroused in me a certain level of respect. There was something about the guy that almost forced me to like him.

After a few weeks, I determined to get rid of the nice, misguided man. The visits seemed pointless to me. So I figured I'd simply level him by bluntly stating my opinion of his God and his religion.

Escorting him from my room to the front door, I prepared myself to blurt out my thoughts about the God-is-love idea. It would be the first time I had ever voiced what was in my head on the matter. I wasn't even sure what I would say.

"Listen, I think it's great that you love God and you *think* He loves you, but I don't buy it at all. It just doesn't add up with reality. I mean 2 + 2 = 4, not 56. And the real world of suffering just doesn't equate with this God-is-love concept."

He was quiet and listening, with what looked like genuine interest in what I had to say. So I continued with my foolproof reasoning.

"I'm not God, and I don't claim to love everyone like you say

He does, but if I saw someone abusing their kid, I'd intervene. If I saw children starving to death, I'd feed them. If I saw a man beating his wife, I'd stop him. I'm not God, and I don't claim to love everyone, but if I had the power to bring all the torment of this messed up world to an end, I'd do it. So don't tell me God loves people. Reality is far more persuasive than religion."

What a relief. It felt so good to put in words the feelings that had churned within me for years. And it all made perfect sense. My logic was airtight, or at least I thought it was.

The youth pastor didn't have an answer for me. But he had something far more important at this moment. He had honesty, a sympathizing honesty. He simply looked at me with eyes that reflected the pain I felt, and said, "Yeah, I agree, it doesn't add up. It's so hard to understand how God can stand by and watch us suffer."

Perhaps I expected some kind of pre-fab religious cliche: "God said it, I believe it, and that settles it for me." For a cultural Christian, born and raised in the church, answers like that might be meaningful—maybe; but not for people who aren't sure if God even exists. Because he didn't give me that kind of answer, my respect level for the youth pastor raised super high in that moment.

Just before walking out the door he had one final thing to say.

"Would you do me one favor? Would you be willing to read just the first chapter of that book," he challenged, pointing over to a three-inch thick volume sitting on my mother's reading table. "Not the whole book, just the first chapter. It may have the answer."

"Sure, I'll read the first chapter."

Looking back, I am amazed that I said *Yes*. I still feel like someone else said *Yes* with my mouth before I could say *No*.

That evening, seventeen years of age and completely skeptical, I sat down alone to fulfill my promise. I read the first chapter of the book. The subject matter had to do with God's character in the light of human suffering. I didn't understand most of what

I read, but one very important thing did dawn on my mind. It was as if someone turned a light on inside of me. Complete mental and emotional revolution occurred in just a few moments of time. Though the book didn't say it in these exact words, a simple, profound picture of reality took shape in my mind:

Love mandates freedom; freedom creates risk; but love is worth the risk.

To this point I had reasoned that love mandated control. If God truly was a being of love and goodness, He would simply not allow evil to exist. And if it ever tried to raise its ugly head, He'd squash it instantly. The least He could do now, since evil has already flourished, would be to destroy all the bad people and start over with the good ones.

But now I was seeing an entirely different picture of love, of God. I could see that love, by its very nature, requires that God grant freedom, and that an absolute control would extinguish in our hearts the capacity for love. And yet, freedom is risky. The same liberty that makes love possible also makes rebellion possible.

Wow!

All I could do was sit there dumbfounded at the elementary beauty of the logic that was now reconstructing my thoughts and feelings. Like waking from a dream, I sensed myself being born into reality as it truly is. That evening I realized that "God is love" (1 John 4:8), and that His love is so genuine and deep that He has no choice but to allow us to love Him in return or not. And if not, the only alternative to love is selfishness, which inevitably leads to injustice and suffering.

Suddenly, God appeared beautiful. I could see Him. Not a face, but a person, a character composed of desirable qualities I had so long wished could exist.

It was as if I were eight years old again, sitting in front of my mother and hearing the words, "He's not your father; your father is someone good and kind." The ugly picture of God I had previously seen in my mind now gave way to an entirely new picture. I met my heavenly Father and liked the Person He turned out to be. I was free. Now I had someone to look up to, a Father worth emulating.

The pages that follow share that picture.

FATHER GOD: *If you had not introduced Yourself to me on that day, I don't know where or what I'd be. But it wouldn't be good. Thank you for finding me in the darkness and leading me into the light. You're so great. I can't wait to meet You face to face. In the name of Jesus Christ, I pray. Amen.*

TWO
WHAT DO YOU SEE?

Your heart is made of canvas.

Is it a

It holds a portrait of God.

beautiful picture?

MY DAUGHTER AMBER looks a lot like me. Once when the two of us were traveling out of the country together, a customs officer questioned our relationship to one another. (Lots of children are abducted.)

"He's my dad," Amber matter-of-factly replied.

"I don't think so," was the officer's stern response. "You look too old to be his daughter and he looks too young to be your father."

Amber did look older than thirteen. And I suppose I did look younger than however old I was at the time. The customs officer was not buying our story. Without speaking a word to one another, both of us got the same idea. We posed a twin-profile for the officer and told her to take a good look at our faces, especially our identical noses.

"Yep, you're definitely related," she smiled and waved us on.

I have attempted to apologize to Amber over the years for her distinct likeness to me. But she doesn't seem to be worried about it. In fact, one time I noticed a new wall-hanging in her bedroom. (It's always interesting to see what a teenager will hang on her walls. Sometimes it can even be a bit scary.) It was a framed photo of me when I was a teenager. (See what I mean?)

"Wow, Amber, you sure look a lot like me when I was a teenager," I said with a big, searching smile.

"Amber," I continued, "does it bother you that you look so much like me?"

I'll never forget her girlish giggle and the answer she gave me.

"No, Daddy, it doesn't bother me. I like looking like you."

"Even the nose, Sweetheart?"

"Yeah, Dad, even the nose." (Don't misunderstand. There's not any real problem with "our" nose. Let's just say we can smell really well. Fortunately, hers is the smaller, female version of mine.)

Those words, "I like looking like you," are some of the most precious ever spoken to me as a father. I think God would find pleasure in hearing words like that from His children. I really do. You know why? Because the absolute highest praise that can be given to any person, including God, is emulation. To want to be like God is the most meaningful expression of reverence and adoration we can offer Him.

But. . .

Right here a serious problem arises.

Would you really want to be like the God you see in your head? Who is He in your mind's eye? What do you see, what do you feel, when you think of God? Is He beautiful in your eyes?

Don't shrug this matter off lightly. Consider carefully the picture of God you hold in your heart. Ultimately you will survive into eternity or fade into oblivion on this vital issue alone. (More on this point later.)

So think with your mind.

Feel with your heart.

Who is God?

Our world is filled with popular pictures of God. Have you noticed?

I met a man in an airport in India who believes he knows who God is. The intense-looking gentleman was dressed in a brightly colored robe and turban. As he sat next to me and began to read a religious book, my curiosity began to peak. I tried to guess in my mind what he might believe.

"Sir," I cautiously addressed him, "would you mind if I asked you a question?"

"Not at all," was his friendly reply. I was at ease.

"I noticed your distinctive clothing and the book you're reading. Are you a religious man?"

"Yes, I am. In fact, I am a *very* religious man, a Universalist monk. My entire life is devoted to the study of God."

"How interesting," I continued. "What exactly do you believe about God? Who is He?"

"An easy question, and one I shall delight to answer, although you should have asked, *What* is God, not *who*. GOD is Generation, Organization and Destruction. God is the universal energy that generates all forms of life. The same God-energy organizes all life into evolving, functional structures. And then God destroys all life."

I couldn't help but probe deeper.

"Is this God a person, with a mind and heart?"

"No, no, not at all," he laughed. "God is far too ruthless and reckless to be a person."

What picture do *you* see when *you* think of God? Is He mindless, heartless energy on a cruel course of evolution and destruction?

While I was in India I encountered another picture of God. As I passed by a shrine, equipped with a very loud speaker system playing chants to draw the people, I paused to watch the worshipers place offerings of food, flowers and money in front of a statue made of paper and plaster. When I asked about its identity, I was told, "She is Kali, goddess of destruction. The offerings are made to calm her wrath and ensure that nothing tragic happens to the worshiper."

Kali is just one of many gods in this view of deity. Most of them are wholly cruel, or at least a confusing mixture of compassion and cruelty. The gods require much and give little. The constant quest of the worshiper is to appease the wrath of the gods by means of religious ceremony, payment of money or good deeds. Strangely, the gods require goodness while they themselves are not good. They carefully note each bad deed and by means of *karma* make bad things happen to the wrongdoer as payback. If you do good, then good things *may* happen to you. Life is an endless effort to be good enough to obtain a higher level of reincarnation on the ascent to personal godhood. If you die in an unholy state, tough luck. You can expect to enter your next life at a lower state—perhaps as a deformed or poverty-stricken person, or even as a despised animal or a bug.

Someone reading this is thinking, "What utter nonsense, those heathen religions. I'm so glad I am a Christian."

Hurrah for the Christians!

Not!

I wish we could say with perfect accuracy that Christianity is immune to false concepts of God. Unfortunately, this is not the case.

One time a Christian friend of mine was going through a period of serious stress in her life. I offered to have prayer with her, to seek God's guidance and help. First I prayed. After saying *amen*, I waited for her to pray. She was silent. Finally I opened my eyes. She was trembling.

"Would you rather not pray?" I asked.

"I want to pray," she explained, "but I just can't pray to God the Father as you have. I would feel more comfortable if we could pray to Jesus instead."

"Why?" I questioned.

"I just don't think the Father will answer our prayers for me. The reason my life is falling apart is because He is punishing me for my sins. But I know Jesus is compassionate. Hopefully He can overrule God's wrath by pleading on my behalf."

Some people see God as a super powerful head-honcho who takes sadistic pleasure in our pain. They think He actually or-chestrates our suffering to punish us for our sins, or worse yet, merely for His own satisfaction; and Jesus is the good guy who may be able to persuade the Father to calm down and be kind.

I heard of a Christian man who got in a serious car accident after losing his temper with his wife. While lying on his hospital bed, his precious Christian wife informed him that God must have pushed his car into the oncoming truck as punishment for his anger toward her.

The visiting pastor said, "Amen! God knows how to bring us around."

The patient in the next bed asked, "I wonder what the guy in the truck is being punished for? For that matter, I wonder what I'm being punished for? Pastor, could you please ask God to lighten up a little?"

Then there's my friend Danny. Christianity is the only religion he has ever known. He's been a constant disappearing act over the years. Every once in a while he resurfaces after plunging into hard drug addiction and sexual decadence. The last time I saw Danny there were tears in his eyes as he opened his heart to me.

"I just can't hold on," he told me with quivering lips.

"Every time I decide to come clean and commit my life to Christ, I feel so good. I have peace. I know it's right. I know it's what I want to do. But after a few weeks, or maybe a month or two at the most, I catch myself overeating or thinking lustful thoughts or feeling angry toward someone. I know the Bible condemns gluttony and says we should be pure in our thoughts. As soon as I fail, I know God can't tolerate it. I feel condemned and rejected by Him. I just can't see how He can keep loving me when I blow it. If I could just keep from sinning, I know He would accept me."

Not a few Christians feel much the same as Danny—God accepts those who are good enough to earn His favor and waits with an attitude of condemnation while the rest of us try to get our acts together.

A rational little boy arrived at a logical conclusion after the sermon at church one day. He said to his parents, "God and Santa Claus must be brothers or something."

"Why do you say that?" his mother inquired.

"Because they both have a big, long list and they're checking it twice and everything depends on whether you're naughty or nice."

A popular radio preacher has deduced the Christian message down to one basic axiom: "Turn or burn." That's his motto. He calls it *the gospel*, which means, *good news*. From this foundation he elaborates with greater depth:

"Turn from your sins, accept Jesus Christ as your personal Savior, or God will imprison you in a fire that will never cease to burn you for all eternity. I suggest you get your act together in a hurry, sinner. And don't forget, God loves you."

This is no fringe belief held by a few kooky Christians. The majority of mainline church folks actually believe that God is presently torturing millions of people who have died and gone to hell, and He will continue to do so forever and ever, daily casting new victims into the flames. We consider men like Hitler and Stalin monsters for less.

Some theological views make atheism look like a good idea.

Contrary to popular Christian opinion, atheism is not the worst thing in the world. Bad religion is. And within the scope of bad religion, bad Christianity is at the top of the list. The reason why is quite obvious. When those who claim to know God best really don't, misrepresentation of the divine character is the inevitable result. Eminent historians have suggested that atheism may very well be the child of the medieval church, born into our world as a reaction to her grotesque picture of God.

Don't get me wrong. Certainly the idea that there is no God is a discouraging thought, rather bleak at best. If there is no God, then we have no future beyond this life. Worse yet, the here-and-now is basically meaningless. All there is to life is an animalistic scratching and clawing for survival with total self-centered gusto.

But wait a minute. At least when it's over, it's over. So atheism is not a worst-case scenario. There is a picture of the great beyond even more gut-wrenching than no God at all. And this particular outlook is not merely bleak; it's downright terrifying.

What if there *is* a God, an actual superior being out there somewhere, but He is not completely good? What if He's an unpredictable mixture of good and evil? If we're alone in the universe, that's bad news. But if the universe is governed by an all-powerful being who is anything less than perfectly good, that's horrifying news. In the darkest recesses of human imagination, no more nightmarish picture could be conjured up. Death would be the passageway into the presence of One whom we could only serve as slaves or despise as rebels. The afterlife would open before us an uncertain realm of arbitrary rule. We would find ourselves in the inescapable control of One whom we could never trust. And the true love for which our hearts so deeply long would turn out to be an utter impossibility.

But consider another possibility.

In the classic Lewis allegory, *Chronicles of Narnia*, God is symbolically represented by a majestic, powerful lion. When four children come to visit the land of Narnia, they hear about the mighty lion ruler, Aslan. With an air of awe and reverence, Mr. and Mrs. Beaver tell them just how mighty He is.

One of the children responds, "I feel rather nervous about meeting a lion."

Mrs. Beaver explains that such nervousness is quite normal: "If there's anyone who can appear before Aslan without their knees knocking, they're either braver than most or else just silly."

"Then he isn't safe?" replies one of the children.

"Safe?" Mr. Beaver giggles. "'Course he isn't safe. But he's good."

Immediately the anxiety of the children is relieved on that assuring note.

What a marvelous and pleasing paradox!

Almighty power in the possession of infinite goodness.

What if there is a God. . .and what if He is infinitely powerful and at the same time infinitely good? One cannot imagine a more comforting, glorious reality!

Suddenly, life would become extremely meaningful.

The character of God matters. He happens to be the Person in charge of the universe, you and me included in that vast domain. Eventually we're going to find ourselves in His immediate presence. Are you looking forward to the encounter?

Think.

Feel.

Who is God?

What do you see?

Is He the kind of person you would want to be like?

It all depends on what you believe He thinks and feels when He looks at you.

GOD: *Whoever You are, make it clear to me. Let me see You for who You really are so I can decide whether I want to be like You or not. Amen.*

THREE

LOOK AGAIN...
FOR THE FIRST TIME

Jesus came to our world to give the

the true character

gift of eternal life by revealing

of God.

A FAVORITE SONG of mine portrays a little girl flying on wings of joy through a field of flowers. She is caught up in the simple, happy thought that Jesus made the beautiful flowers for her enjoyment.

In open fields of wild flowers,
She breathes the air and flies away.
She thanks her Jesus
for the daisies and the roses
in no simple language.

And yet, her perception of God is small. She doesn't really know who He is. He is more, far more than her childish heart has yet grasped. Sometime in the future, as she grows up in understanding, she will see Him as He really is. Then, an intelligent trust will be born in her heart.

Someday she'll understand the meaning of it all.
He's more than the laughter
or the stars in the heavens;
As close as a heartbeat
or a song on her lips.
Some day she'll trust Him
and learn how to see Him.

Seeing God for Who He really is, and trusting Him because of what she sees, she falls in love with Him.

Someday He'll call her,
and she will come running
and fall in His arms,
and the tears will fall down and she'll pray,

I want to fall in love with You.
I want to fall in love with You.
I want to fall in love with You.
(Written by Dan Haseltine.)

We are incapable of loving God unless we can first trust Him. And we cannot trust Him unless we see Him. . .unless we truly see Him as He is, as One who can be trusted because of who He is. All distorted images tend toward distrust and extinguish in the soul the capacity to love God. All clarity of God's character leads toward trust, which in turn gives birth to love in the soul. This is the most basic of all principles regarding human relationship with God.

Where then do we find perfect clarity? The Bible gives only one answer: "The very God who commanded the light to shine out of darkness has illuminated our hearts by giving the light of the knowledge of His true character in the person of Jesus Christ" (2 Corinthians 4:6; personal translation). Another passage of Scripture explains that Jesus is "the brightness of God's glory [character] and the express image of His person [who God is and what He's like]" (Hebrews 1:3).

If we want to see God clearly, we need to look at Jesus.
Not at religion.
Not at any other person.
Not at our own experiences in life.
Not even at any isolated doctrinal truth outside of the illuminating context of Christ.

"For the law was given through Moses, but grace and truth came through Jesus Christ. No one has seen God [clearly] at any time. The only begotten Son, who is in the bosom [heart] of the Father, He has declared Him" (John 1:17, 18, NKJV).

In Christ alone do we encounter God with perfect clarity. All other media are dim at best and completely distorted at worst.

Shortly before His crucifixion, Jesus prayed an extremely significant and revealing prayer. The Savior spelled out the vital nature of His mission on earth as the incarnation of Deity. Here, like no other place in Scripture, we are ushered into the inner chamber of divine thought and purpose for humanity.

Jesus opened His passionate prayer by defining the eternal life He came to give: "This is eternal life, that they may know You, the only true God, and Jesus Christ whom You have sent" (John 17:3, NKJV).

Notice that Jesus did not define eternal life in terms of its *duration*, but rather in terms of its *quality*. He did not say, "Eternal life is to live forever." That's a given. Certainly eternal life involves an endless length of living. But Jesus says, *Eternal life is to know the only true God as He is revealed in the One whom He has sent—Jesus Christ.* This is why the apostle John could say that eternal life is the possession of the believer in this present life: "You may know that you *have* [present tense] eternal life" (1 John 5:13, NKJV). We may have eternal life here and now, while we are in the process of dying. Many people throughout history have died while possessing eternal life, because eternal life is a quality of life that derives its essence from knowing God.

Understanding who God really is, seeing His true character distinct from all false pictures, is the psychological and emotional substance of which eternal life is composed. Knowing God heals the soul of all internal maladies and imparts a quality of life that is *eternal.* There is earth-transcending peace to be derived from knowing that the One who made us, and to whom we are ultimately accountable, is infinitely and intrinsically good. On the other hand, all false pictures of God are destructive to the soul, eating away the beauty and meaning of life.

Upon this foundation Jesus built His prayer. If knowing God is eternal life, certainly the purpose of the Savior's mission to our world would be to make known God's true character. Notice how His prayer continues:

"I have glorified You on the earth. I have finished the work which You have given Me to do. . . I have manifested Your name" (John 17:4, 6, NKJV).

By His own testimony, the specific work Jesus came to our world to accomplish was to glorify God and manifest His name.

The word *glory* in Scripture is rooted in the concept of *divine self-disclosure*. When Moses asked the Lord, "Please, show me Your *glory*," the Lord answered, "I will make all My *goodness* pass before you" (Exodus 33:18, 19, NKJV). In response to the request of Moses to see God's glory, the Lord proclaimed the goodness of His character. Hence the *glory* of God is His *character*.

Similarly, the word *name* may be literally translated *character*. In the Bible, names often carry the meaning of specific attributes by which individuals are known. *Jacob*, for example, means *deceiver*. But when he struggled through his guilt and laid hold of God's forgiveness, his name was changed to *Israel*, which means *one who has prevailed with God*.

So when Jesus said He had accomplished His work by glorifying God and manifesting His name, we are to understand that His work on earth was to reveal and magnify God's true character. In so doing, He gave to the world the gift of eternal life. We become experiential partakers of the free gift of eternal life by seeing and believing the revelation, by accepting into the mind and emotions the true and accurate picture of God's character of love manifested in Christ. The revelation is namely this: That God in Christ reached out of Himself to redeem sinners while they were yet in their sins, wholly by the intrinsic goodness of His grace and not in response to any right doing on our part (see Titus 3:4, 5; 2 Timothy 1:9, 10). This monumental achievement found expression in the incarnation, life, death and resurrection of the Son of God. By condescending to become one with the human race, by living a sinless life as one of us, and bearing all our sin before we did anything at all to merit the saving overture, Christ made known the selfless beauty of the Father's love. When we encounter that revelation, believing that what we see in Jesus is the true picture of God, salvation becomes our personal experience. We are saved by the revelation of God's character, which is the same as saying we are saved "by grace" (Ephesians 2:8). For grace is, in simple terms, God's character of love manifested toward undeserving sinners. Our part is to allow the truth of God's love to awaken faith within us, which enables us to embrace the revelation (see Galatians 5:6).

As Jesus continued His prayer, He said something astounding about God's character: "Thou hast…loved them, as Thou hast loved Me" (John 17:23). Here is the heart of God. Here is His grace. He loves fallen sinners, the likes of you and me, just as He loves Jesus, the sinless One.

Do you realize what this means?

If God loves you and me, fallen sinners, with just as much passion and depth as He loves Jesus, the Sinless One, then we can only conclude that His love must transcend the dark reality of our sinfulness. Our sin does not alter, lessen or put off His love. It is a changeless, undying love that cannot be quenched by sin's ugliness. It must be a love, as well, that predates any good deeds that we may do, and is, in fact, the only means by which good deeds that are truly good may be achieved in our lives. Because God loves us in our sinfulness, just as He loves Jesus in His sinlessness, we must believe that His love is a constant, immovable reality that is not dependent on our goodness. Rather, we are utterly dependent on the revelation of God's love to generate any real goodness in us.

The final words of Jesus' prayer pinpoint our world's fundamental problem and highlight God's saving solution:

"O righteous Father! The world has not known You, but I have known You; and these have known that You sent Me. And I have declared to them Your name, and will declare it, that the love with which You have loved Me may be in them, and I in them" (John 17:25, 26, NKJV).

Jesus addresses the Father as *righteous*, meaning His character is composed of good and love-motivated attributes. God is beautiful. His heart is filled with nothing other than infinite love. This is how the Son of God sees His Father. And yet the Savior laments that the world does not see God in this light. Human beings generally do not know who God is or what He is like. False conceptions of Deity abound in the hearts of men and women and children. We see a God of force who arbitrarily imposes His will. We see a God who turns His love on and off according to our successes and failures. We see a God who orchestrates the tragedies that bring us heartache and pain. We see a God who is swift to pounce with punishment and slow to favor with forgiveness. In our sin-distorted imaginations we see an ugly, unattractive God whom we can only despise with the spite of rebels or serve with the anxiety of slaves.

And yet, there is a Light that shines in our darkness. There is One who knows God and has made Him known. Meditating on the success of His fragile expedition to earth, Jesus summarized His glorious achievement by saying to His Father, *They don't know You as You really are; but I do, and I have made You known to them. This I have done so they can experience Your love for them as I have experienced Your love for Me.* On that note the prayer closes. His mission to the world is unmistakably defined.

All the healing miracles of the Savior's ministry. All the teaching and touching and tender loving. All the reckless mercy and the careful justice. And finally, the self-abandoning sacrifice on the cross. All of it was meant for one premeditated purpose: to reveal the powerful beauty of the Father's character of love.

FATHER GOD: *Jesus has made it abundantly clear that I am lost because I do not know You. He has made it equally clear that I shall be healed of sin's power by seeing the revelation of Your character in Him. Knowing You is the essence of eternal life. May the light of the knowledge of Your sin-transcending love flood my heart as I continue to encounter Christ, in whose name I pray. Amen.*

FOUR

HOW GOD LOOKS
IN THE DARK

It's really **dark** in here.

Would someone turn on the light?

WE DON'T USUALLY ASSOCIATE darkness with God. When we speak of darkness in a spiritual sense, we are referring to the devil and his evil empire. Of the Creator, Scripture declares, "God is light, and in Him is no darkness at all" (1 John 1:5). You can imagine my perplexity, then, when I read a Bible passage that put God in the darkness rather than in the light. Contemplating God, King David declared, "Clouds and darkness surround Him. . ." (Psalm 97:2, NKJV).

Obviously this passage is not speaking of literal darkness. God dwells in the presence of millions of angels who radiate with dazzling brightness. So what kind of darkness could possibly surround the One who lives in "unapproachable light?" (1 Timothy 6:16, NKJV).

We get a clue by reading the whole verse:

"Clouds and darkness surround Him; righteousness and justice are the foundation of His throne."

A contrast is here drawn between *darkness* and *righteousness*. *Righteousness* is a character word, defining thoughts and feelings and behavior. Therefore, the *darkness* here mentioned must also be a character word. The inspired writer says, in essence, "Darkness surrounds the character of God, but the fact is that righteousness is the true essence of His Character." God may look bad to us, but in reality He's good. There is a kind of spiritual darkness that clouds our ideas about God. However, that darkness is present in our perception and does not arise out of His true identity. We don't see God as He really is. Somehow, by some means, we humans have come to view His character in a false light.

But how? And what is the nature of this darkness?

Human perception of the divine character was first distorted in the hearts and minds of our original parents, Adam and Eve. The account given in Scripture is very enlightening.

Basically what happened was this: God's archenemy, Satan, told Adam and Eve a two-pronged lie about God's character. (1) God cannot be trusted (2) because He is totally self-serving and does not have your best interest at heart. Satan painted a new picture of God, and we became rebels by believing that dark portrait. Notice how the father of lies framed his case against the Creator:

"Now the Serpent was more subtil than any beast of the field which the Lord God had made. And he said unto the woman, Yea, hath God said, Ye shall not eat of every tree of the garden? And the woman said unto the serpent, We may eat of the fruit of the trees of the garden: but of the fruit of the tree which is in the midst of the garden, God hath said, Ye shall not eat of it, neither shall ye touch it, lest ye die. And the serpent said unto the woman, Ye shall not surely die: for God doth know that in the day ye eat thereof, then your eyes shall be opened, and ye shall be as gods, knowing good and evil" (Genesis 3:1-5).

The first thing we want to notice is the word *subtil* in verse one. Satan approached with an intent to deceive, to lead humanity to believe an untruth about God.

Don't overlook the underlying point of his falsehood. Read between the lines. When Satan uttered the words, "Yea, hath God said?..." he placed a question mark on God's word, bringing His very integrity under suspicion. He communicated into the human heart an idea of mistrust toward the Lord. Then he proceeded to blatantly contradict what God had said: "Ye shall not surely die." The insinuation is evident: *I know God said you'll die if you eat this fruit, but I'm telling you no such thing will happen. God is a liar. He cannot be trusted.*

If that wasn't bad enough, the next thing Satan said made the lie even more dark and tempting: *The whole reason why God has lied to you is because He knows that if you eat this desirable fruit you'll be exalted to equality with Him. He is totally selfish and doesn't want you to break up His monopoly on this higher state of freedom and pleasure. He doesn't love you. He only cares about Himself. Break free from His tyrannical rule.*

On the inner canvas of human imagination Satan painted God in his own ugly image, in the dark hues of dishonesty and selfishness. Because the temptation was woven out of a subtle misrepresentation of God's character, the sin problem is far deeper than mere behavioral misconduct. When Adam and Eve partook of the forbidden fruit, they had, in effect, believed what Satan said about God. As a result, their perception of God's character was drastically altered. Whereas once they believed Him to be a God of infinite love who desired their eternal happiness, now they believed He was untrustworthy and self-serving.

It is here, at the level of perception and belief that the darkening of God's character occurred in the human soul. We now imagine our Maker to be someone He is not, and that distorted picture has deeply wounded our capacity to relate to God with love and trust. This is why the Bible defines sin in terms of its effect on our relationship with God and our ability to see Him clearly: "Your iniquities have separated you from your God; and your sins have hidden His face from you" (Isaiah 59:2, NKJV). God has not arbitrarily rejected mankind and angrily turned away. Rather, sin has imposed upon the human heart an emotional and psychological barrier that separates us from God. Sin itself, by virtue of what it is, has hidden God's character from our hearts and minds. Because of sin, there are things we believe about God that are not true. Sin is a deceptive, dimming influence that clouds our perception of the One who made us. The rest of the story explains, in psychological terms, how sin does this to us.

The immediate effect of sin on Adam and Eve was to awaken in them a sense of condemnation and guilt: "The eyes of them both were opened, and they knew that they were naked" (Genesis 3:7). The *eyes* here mentioned are not the literal eyeballs with which we see our physical surroundings, but rather a metaphor to indicate the inner eyes of conscience with which we sense either guilt or innocence. Adam and Eve became conscious of their wrongdoing and began to experience the psychological phenomenon of guilt.

Notice what happened next: "And they heard the voice of the Lord God walking in the garden in the cool of the day; and Adam and his wife hid themselves from the presence of the Lord God amongst the trees of the garden" (Genesis 3:8).

Strange, new impulse! Those who just yesterday felt completely comfortable in God's presence now feel a compelling drive to hide from Him.

"And the Lord God called unto Adam, and said unto him, Where art thou?" (Genesis 3:9). As if God didn't know the exact tree they were hiding behind. Of course He knew where they were, but He approached with a gentle wooing calculated to reconcile rather than further alienate. The fact that Adam and Eve willingly came out of their hiding place indicates that God's tone of voice and attitude must have been flooded with compassion rather than condemnation.

When Adam spoke to the Lord he revealed the source of their new impulse to hide: "I heard Thy voice in the garden, and I was afraid, because I was naked; and I hid myself" (Genesis 3:10).

Afraid of God?

But why?

They were never afraid of Him before.

Had God changed in some way?

No!

"For I am the Lord, I change not" (Malachi 3:6). "The same yesterday, and today, and forever" (Hebrews 13:8). He still loved them and cared for them just the same. But *they* had changed. Now they could not see His goodness. The natural result of sin is to exclude man from God's love from man's perspective. Those feelings are directly derived from the effect of sin itself upon the conscience, they are not arbitrarily imposed by an attitude of condemnation assumed by God. He remains unchanged, but sin changes us. Our sin does not alter God's love, rather it erects a wall of separation for which our sin is the cause, not God.

Take note of the fact that Adam and Eve were afraid of God because of the guilt they felt inside themselves. Here is a crucial key to understanding the sin problem. Because sin involved embracing a distorted view of God's character, they imagined that the condemnation they felt was proceeding from God. Hence, they were afraid of Him. They could no longer sense His love and acceptance due to the deceptive influence of their rebellion. Sin is a reality-blurring force, bringing dark emotions into the soul. It presses the mind to see God in a false light. It tells the heart that God rejects and condemns the sinner along with the sin. Shattered innocence, leading to a confused mixture of self-hatred and self-justification, is organic to sin's very nature. God does condemn sin. He cannot do otherwise. But He continues to love the sinner. The condemnation we feel is in the sin, not in God.

While God is the architect of conscience, He is not the author of condemnation and guilt. The way we feel toward others and ourselves in response to sin is not an accurate reflection of God's thoughts and feelings toward us. "If our heart condemn us, God is greater than our heart, and knoweth all things" (1 John 3:20). In other words, we need to look beyond the condemnation in our hearts and see that God's love is a more powerful reality than the guilt sin imposes on us. He knows everything about us, and yet He loves us still. There is no more liberating consciousness than this. To know and believe that God loves us without condemnation, even though He knows everything about us and hates our sin, frees us from the power inherent in our guilt to continue holding us in hopeless bondage. Any religious ideology that pictures God as the source of condemnation toward the sinner is incapable of breaking the grip of sin. For as long as the inner eyes of perception and conscience cannot see God's intrinsic goodness and infinite love, lavished upon us while we are yet sinners, sin will continue to masquerade as our liberation and God will continue to appear as our enslaving enemy. Apart from a true knowledge of God's character of love, we have only one of two options: either rebellion against God or fearful slavery to a false conception of God.

Guilt is cleansed away when we see and believe that the very
One who *could* condemn, *does not*. When God's pardoning grace
looms in our minds larger than our sin, then we see sin for what
it really is and God for who He really is. Sin loses its spell-bind-
ing influence. When we understand that God's love is not with-
drawn in response to our wrongdoing—when we see and believe
this reality—the glad tidings neutralize our shame and recon-
struct the true image of God in the soul. We are healed by that
true image.

This is not positive thinking. It is the truth. God does not
condemn us. He does, in actual fact, continue to love us in spite
of our sin. Non-condemnatory love is the static, changeless reality of God's beautiful character. To see God in this healing light,
as He really is, absorbs the paralyzing poison of our guilt and
breaks our affinity with sin.

I am guilty. No doubt about it.

God hates my sin, because it hurts me, the one He loves. This
is clear.

But I am not condemned by God.

He loves me because He is good, not because I'm good.

What a relief!

The rebellion is gone.

Now I can live.

And now I want to be good, like Him.

FATHER: *Sin has really messed me up. It has seriously damaged my
inner capacity to see Your true character clearly. I am naturally afraid
of You because of my guilt. Somehow sin has twisted things around
in my mind, pressuring me to believe that You condemn me and
cannot love me. A clear sense of Your forgiving mercy is my only
hope. Heal me by Your love as I behold Your character. I am looking
for You in Christ. Amen.*

FIVE
HOW GOD LOOKS
IN THE MIRROR

That window in your heart . . . through

it's a mirror.

which you think you **see** God . . .

I ONCE SAW GOD,
    As through a window in my soul I peered.
He was just as I suspected,
    Just as I feared.
So selfish and cruel
    He appeared to be;
So very ugly,
    So unlike me.
Then looked I deeper,
    Still deeper with time;
T'was a mirror all along,
    And the image was mine.

God makes a very penetrating observation about us humans:
"These things you have done, and I kept silent; *you thought that I was altogether like you*; but I will rebuke you, and set them [your sins] in order [as they really are] before your eyes" (Psalm 50:21, NKJV).

Inherent in sin is guilt. But the sinful heart naturally tries to evade its guilt by shifting blame to others, and ultimately to God. We like to take comfort in the self-soothing idea that we are no worse than anyone else, and probably better than most. The problem runs deeper still as we project our fallen image onto God. We tend to imagine that He is like us, crediting to Him our own evil attributes. We have "changed the glory [character] of the uncorruptible God into an image made like to corruptible man" (Romans 1:23).

Our assumption that God's character is like ours has a reason behind it, though we rarely face that reason with humble honesty. In the darkest recesses of our fallen psyche we are driven by an unconscious desire to pull Him down so that we might be lifted up. "Wilt thou condemn Me," the Lord puts His finger on the sensitive nerve, "that thou mayest be righteous?" (Job 40:8). If He looks bad, then we look good, or at least not so bad after all. No need to face our guilt and bow before Him if He is not innocent and holy in our eyes. We blame Him in a self-centered attempt at self-justification. Humanity is possessed of a guilt-driven motive to fabricate an image of God that resembles ourselves in order to evade reality—the painful, healing reality that God is infinitely good in stark contrast to our sinfulness. If we were to believe that He is wholly righteous, our own ugliness would appear in its true light as completely unjustifiable—the pain. And yet, we would see God as He really is—the healing.

Projecting our guilt outward, onto others and onto God, is one of the original characteristics of the sin problem as it began in Eden. Adam blamed Eve. Eve blamed the serpent (*the devil made me do it*). Ultimately they were both blaming God, since God made Eve and the serpent. The only other alternative would have been to take full responsibility for their sin and believe that God was good enough to forgive. That route was obviously too painful to tread, so they opted for casting blame. As one of the tragic legacies of the fall, human beings have been blaming one another and God ever since Eden.

Attributing to God the evil and tragedy that torments our world acts as a psychological buffer of sorts to hide the fact that we are responsible, that all the suffering which bludgeons our race is the direct result of our own sin. We shake our culpable fist at Him as a kind of emotional survival mechanism. And because He is a God of selfless love, He has no choice but to allow our misconceptions of His character to cloud our vision of Him for a time. His only alternative would be to fully disclose His total innocence and goodness, which would, in contrast, fully expose our true guilt. If allowed to dawn upon us with immediate, perfect clarity, the full reality of God's love and righteousness would destroy us with the undiluted guilt that would naturally come upon us. In order to save us from that lethal guilt, God self-sacrificingly allows the total truth of His holiness to be hidden behind the blame we so desperately heap upon Him.

And yet, He is not completely silent. For He knows that our full redemption is possible only through the revelation of His glorious love. He cannot, and will not, forever remain shrouded in the darkness of our twisted perceptions. He takes full responsibility for our sin and suffering, bearing our blame with grace, while simultaneously revealing His love and goodness in healing doses, rather than in one megadose of destructive magnitude. In His wise and compassionate plan, "Now we see through a glass, darkly. . . ."

However, the darkness is not friend, but foe, although it is tolerated for a time that we might be purified by gradual revelation. "Now we see through a glass, darkly; but then face to face: now I know in part; but then shall I know even as also I am known" (1 Corinthians 13:12). God leads His children on, step by step, until they finally see and know Him, and themselves, as He knows. Perfect honesty is the ultimate end to which our redemption is tending.

Oswald Chambers observed that "A person's character determines how he interprets God's will" (*My Utmost for His Highest*, April 26). He then points his readers to Psalm 18:25, 26 as proof of this psychological phenomenon in human experience: "With the merciful Thou [God] wilt shew Thyself merciful; with the upright man Thou wilt shew Thyself upright; with the pure Thou wilt shew Thyself pure; and with the froward Thou wilt shew Thyself froward."

As with our opening Scripture for this chapter, this passage suggests that we tend to interpret God's character out of our own. If we are merciful in our dealings with others, we will have the perceptual wherewithal to see God's mercy toward ourselves. If we are morally upright and pure in our own hearts and lives, we will be better able to perceive God's character as upright and pure.

On the other hand, if we are "froward (crooked, perverse)" in our characters, we distort our mental and emotional capacity to see and believe that God is pure and merciful. We tend to regard Him as "froward" like us. Who we are in character acts as an internal lens that colors our discernment of God's character. A good camera takes good pictures. A bad camera takes bad pictures.

Jesus communicated this principle in the following two statements:

"Except a man be born again, he cannot *see* the kingdom of God" (John 3:3).

"Blessed are the pure in heart: for they shall *see* God" (Matthew 5:8).

In both of these Scriptures the word *see* refers, not to optical vision, but to perceptual vision, comprehension, understanding. Only those who are "born again" into a spiritual rebirth can understand the principles that govern the divine kingdom. Only those who pursue purity of heart are capable of discerning the truth of God's character.

Are we then to attain personal purity before we can know God to any degree?

This is one of those matters concerning which the question is appropriate, "Which comes first, the chicken or the egg?" We might ask, "Which comes first, the revelation of God's character or the transformation of our characters?" The Bible seems to suggest that there is a sense in which both are true and needful.

On the one hand, we are dependent on the truth of God's goodness penetrating our hearts in order to repent of our sins and be born again (see Romans 2:4; 1 John 4:19). We cannot purify ourselves apart from at least an elementary-level understanding of God's merciful love.

On the other hand, as the revelation begins to dawn upon our hearts, movement toward the light creates an emotional climate in the soul in which greater enlightenment may occur. "In Your light we see light" (Psalm 36:9, NKJV). As we embrace each ray of divine beauty that penetrates our minds, the eyes of our perception adjust to the light and our vision is sharpened. "The path [the spiritual journey] of the just is like the shining sun, that shines ever brighter unto the perfect day" (Proverbs 4:18, NKJV).

When, with sincere desire to know God, we allow our characters to be shaped by the light He gives, we place ourselves in a spiritual condition that makes further discernment of God's character possible. With each progressive revelation and each corresponding reception of the light, we become simultaneously more and more free from misconceptions of the divine character and from our own character deformities. Our perception of Him and our growing likeness to Him dovetail as one process. The revelation and the transformation are concurrent. Finally, "when He shall appear [at the Second Coming of Christ], we shall be like Him; for we shall see Him as He is" (1 John 3:2).

When we deny divine revelation, our transformation ceases and we turn toward any false conception that may be convenient or appropriate for masking our denial. If sin is cherished rather than given up in the light of God's love, the light grows dim until darkness sets in. And when our eyes adjust to the darkness, we think we can see and end up believing that our darkness is the light. Describing this psychological tragedy, Scripture speaks of those who "call evil good, and good evil; that put darkness for light, and light for darkness" (Isaiah 5:20).

In His wise providence, God has allowed the Scriptures to be composed in such a way that those who search its pages with an honest desire to know Him will see His true character shining through. Conversely, the same source of light is a snare of delusion to those who would rather fashion God in their own image in order to evade their personal need to be fashioned into His image. This is the sublime truth Jesus referred to when He said, "For judgment I am come into this world, that they which see not might see; and that they which see might be made blind" (John 9:39). Jesus does not here mean to say that He desires some to see and others to be blind. Rather, He simply describes two possible responses to the light. "For every one that doeth evil hateth the light, neither cometh to the light, lest his deeds should be reproved. But he that doeth truth cometh to the light, that his deeds may be made manifest, that they are wrought in God" (John 3:20, 21).

No human being will ever find the true knowledge of God by looking into himself. The perceptual window in our hearts, through which we think we see Him, is not a window at all, but a mirror that tells lies. "The heart is deceitful above all things, and desperately wicked" (Jeremiah 17:9). We must look out of ourselves to see the Father. Out of ourselves to the One true portrait of the divine character. Out of ourselves to Jesus Christ, who declared of Himself, "I am the way [to God], the truth [about God], and the life [of God]: no man cometh unto the Father, but by Me. . . . He that hath seen Me hath seen the Father" (John 14:6, 9).

> I now see God,
>   As to His Son I gaze;
> So beautiful with goodness
>   Are all of His ways.
> As I continue to look deeper,
>   Still deeper with time,
> His character of love
>   Finds a mirror in mine.

FATHER IN HEAVEN: *Truly You have spoken straight to me. Forgive me for thinking You are like me. Forgive me for attributing my own evil character traits to You. But thank You for so graciously bearing my reproach and blame in order to preserve my sanity, indeed, my very existence. Guide me out of myself into the glorious light of Your Son. Teach me what You are really like as I look to Him. I pray in His name. Amen.*

SIX

THE AWAKENING KISS

To be fully known and yet fully

redemptive

loved is the essence of our

healing.

IN MY FOURTH GRADE CLASS I heard the enchanting story of *Sleeping Beauty*. At least the teacher said it was supposed to be enchanting. I thought it was lame. What a tragedy, I reasoned in my pre-pubertal mind, that the pretty lady could only be awakened from her potentially endless sleep by a yucky kiss from some prince-charming dude. My opinion about kissing sure did change when I finally grew up and met my own sleeping beauty, minus the sleeping part. It's been one of our favorite things to do for nearly twenty years now.

I was intrigued to discover in Scripture a divine kiss, far more powerful and awakening than any human kiss, fact or fiction. It is the kiss of God Almighty, lovingly bestowed upon the entire human race in the divine-human person of Jesus Christ. Tucked away in an Old Testament prophecy concerning the Messiah, we find the healing salvation of God symbolized by a kiss:

"Mercy and truth are met together; righteousness and peace have kissed each other" (Psalm 85:10).

From a biblical perspective, the character of God may be viewed as a delicately poised balance between justice and mercy. Of course there are endless attributes that compose God's character, as there are multiple facets to a diamond. But there is one Bible word that embodies the whole ocean of the divine character. That word is *love*. The apostle John declares, "God is love" (1 John 4:8). While His love encompasses many beautiful qualities, it is composed of two basic hemispheres: justice and mercy. His love is perfectly just and at the same time perfectly merciful.

Justice: "He is the Rock, His work is perfect; for all His ways are justice, a God of truth and without injustice; righteous and upright is He" (Deuteronomy 32:4, NKJV).

Mercy: "Through the Lord's mercies we are not consumed, because His compassions fail not. They are new every morning; great is Your faithfulness" (Lamentations 3:22, 23, NKJV).

The Bible is the story of God's maintaining the vital harmony that must exist between justice and mercy as He endeavors to save fallen human beings. On the one hand, the righteousness of God's character demands that He uphold the truth and justice of His eternal law. On the other hand, the mercy of His character causes Him to be equally desirous to save those who have rebelled against His law.

It may appear as though the Creator is in a dilemma of sorts. If He were to lay aside the just claims of His law in order to save sinners, sin would be excused and could never be conquered. Its influence would spread suffering and destruction throughout the universe. If He were to uphold His law without extending mercy, on the other hand, not one fallen human could be saved. Because God loves sinners but at the same time hates sin, He must somehow maintain His justice while pouring forth His saving mercy.

Really God has no dilemma at all, for there is no conflict between the two dimensions of His character. No dichotomy exists between justice and mercy. They are both expressions of one harmonious character of love. Ultimately justice and mercy are so closely united that they are nearly indistinguishable. One does not cancel out the other. Both are eternal principles that co-exist in the heart of God with perfect equilibrium.

Jesus came into our world to give the kiss of God, to wed justice and mercy together as one in human experience, to manifest the glory of God's infinitely righteous and compassionate character. Of Him Scripture testifies:

"The Word became flesh, and dwelt among us, and we beheld His glory [character], the glory as of the only begotten of the Father, full of grace and truth" (John 1:14).

Notice here that Jesus is described as the embodiment of the Father's character, a character complete in two vital, balancing qualities: *grace and truth* (which is the same as saying, *mercy and justice*). Jesus came to our world clothed with the garb of our humanity (*the word became flesh*) so that we could encounter God's character and survive the stunning ordeal. In Christ we see the perfect holiness of God's character subdued to a tolerable level by virtue of His incarnation in the familiar environment of our own human nature.

The *grace* of God seen in Christ makes it possible for the *truth* of His holiness to be assimilated into our human experience in healing rather than destructive doses. If God were to reveal the pure, unveiled truth of His justice without simultaneously bathing that revelation in mercy, the natural sense of condemnation inherent in our sin would destroy us at the psychological and emotional level. In Christ, justice is tempered by mercy so that the sinner may bear its flawless glory. But be warned: a persistent rejection of God's mercy places the soul in conflict with the claims of justice. And in that conflict, the sinner loses. Those who fully and finally cast aside God's grace will find themselves facing the raw energy of justice with no way of escape.

Understanding and appreciating God's mercy prepares the mind to endure the revelation of His justice. Those who move toward God's mercy are engaging in a process of gradual revelation of God's holy character, and, in natural contrast, exposure of their own sin-damaged characters. If the revelation were allowed to burst upon the soul without the buffer mercy affords, the sinful heart would melt with condemnation. But while mercy is in full view, justice can be brought to bear upon the heart without crushing the sinner. The realization of God's mercy allows the sinner to face his sin and lay it aside by confession and repentance. Free and lavish mercy is the means, the only means, by which the Lord brings about harmony with His justice in the human heart. Mercy alone, in the form of unreserved forgiveness, is of sufficient beauty and power to turn the soul from its sin toward obedience to the just principles of the divine law.

In the final analysis, once the great war between good and evil is over, it will have been made self-evident that God employs

only one power, a single omnipotent influence, in all His rela-
tions with created beings. The Father of the universe continually
pours forth an endless river of love to all, which will eventually
prove to be either eternal life or utter destruction to every person.
Never does anything contrary to His love proceed from Him,
and the intent of that love is always to give and sustain life, never
to destroy. And yet, the very constancy of His love makes it either
healing or horrible. Healing to those who embrace it, because the
love of God cleanses the heart of its guilt and shame. Horrible to
those who reject it, because the very same love cannot avoid draw-
ing attention to the infinite contrast which exists between itself
and human sinfulness.

With unerring accuracy and unswerving consistency the
Creator operates His universe in perfect harmony with the
eternal principles of love inherent in His very nature. It is a love
both just and merciful, with "no variableness neither shadow of
turning" (James 1:17). God is "the same yesterday, and today,
and forever" (Hebrews 13:8). He is not schizophrenic. There is
no polarity or conflict in His mind. Complete accord exists between His justice and His mercy. He exercises mercy with His
justice in view, knowing that those who truly receive His mercy
will seek harmony with the just principles by which He governs
all life. Acceptance of His mercy always tends the heart toward
righteousness. Those who embrace God's mercy for sin inevitably fall in love with Him and seek to incorporate the principles of
His law into their lives. Such is the captivating, transforming effect of divine grace when it is perceived and believed.

King Solomon expressed the matter like this: "By mercy and
truth iniquity is purged" (Proverbs 16:6). Only by the blending of
both mercy and truth can iniquity be cleansed from the human
heart. Mercy alone would produce a liberal contempt for God.
Justice alone would arouse a retaliating rebellion against Him. Only
as we discern in His character the beautiful balance of compassion
and strength, forgiveness and law, grace and truth, will we willingly turn from sin and embrace His law with loyal devotion.

We conclude, then, that sin's power is broken by means of

revelation, by the enlightenment of the mind and emotions concerning the true character of God. When we see and believe the love that God has toward us, sin loses its hold on our hearts. We fall in love with Him and turn from rebellion to allegiance.

To give this vital revelation, the eternal Father sent forth His Son, who alone could manifest the divine character with perfect accuracy. Jesus came near to us in our fallen, needy state, "full of grace and truth," complete in mercy and justice. As we read of the various encounters He had with people, we cannot help but be struck by the fact that He was extremely magnetic. People were drawn to Him.

Why?

Because there is nothing more healing to the sinful heart than to be fully known and yet fully loved. Those who met Jesus sensed that He knew everything about them and still loved them. They knew that He knew every dark secret and every fragile fear lurking in their hearts, and yet He did not condemn. He was full of both "grace and truth." In Him "righteousness and peace have kissed each other." He loves the sinner while hating the sin, and He only hates the sin because it hurts the sinner He loves.

On one occasion Jesus was near a well with no way to draw out water. A Samaritan woman came to the well to fill her containers. Jesus asked if she would give Him a drink. She was startled because He was a Jew and she a Samaritan. "'How is it that You, being a Jew, ask a drink from me, a Samaritan woman?' For Jews have no dealings with Samaritans" (John 4:9, NKJV). But Jesus had no regard for cultural prejudice. He loved this woman regardless of her race.

Then Jesus asked her to do something that aroused her conscience: "Go," He said, "call your husband, and come here" (John 4:16, NKJV). At this point, no doubt, her eyes shifted away from His. Perhaps her mind was racing to find a way to change the subject. "If He only knew," she must have reasoned, "He wouldn't even be talking to me."

But He did know. Every detail!

"The woman answered and said, 'I have no husband.' Jesus

said to her, 'You have well said, 'I have no husband,' for you have had five husbands, and the one whom you now have is not your husband; in that you spoke truly" (John 4:17, 18, NKJV).

Imagine how she must have felt inside. Here was a man she had never met, and yet He knew the unsavory details of her broken life. A sense of truth and justice was bearing down upon her. And yet, somehow, she did not feel like fleeing from His presence. To the contrary, she rushed to her village and said, "Come, see a Man who told me all things I ever did. Could this be the Christ?" (John 4:29, NKJV). She was deeply attracted to Him rather than repelled, and she wanted others to meet Him as well.

Why?

Because He was "full of grace and truth."

Because to be fully known and yet fully loved is the essence of redemption.

Because His healing kiss was upon her.

Even though He knew all about her, she felt that He did not despise her for the life of sin she was living. Such love gives the inner courage and the restored self-respect necessary to turn away from sin and live above its power. In Christ, "mercy and truth have met together; righteousness and peace have kissed each other" (Psalm 85:10).

Have you ever been kissed by God?

I really hope you have.

Because you're a sleeping beauty, whether you know it or not.

Receive His kiss. . .believe He loves you while knowing everything about you. Once you do, you'll find yourself awakening to His beauty and experiencing the pleasure of His lovely image taking shape in your own heart and life.

Kiss me, beloved Lord. *Oh, how I need to experience the simultaneous power of Your grace and truth. Exalt Jesus before my inner eyes of understanding that I may discern the beautiful harmony of Your justice and mercy. I realize You know everything about me, and yet You love me still. This is my awakening. This is my hope. Praise You! I pray in the light of Your Son's lovely character. Amen.*

SEVEN
BLIND IN THE LIGHT

"If all it takes is a willingness to suffer a few

savior, then I could be your

hours of physical pain in order to be a

savior and you could be mine."

I WAS A YOUNG, new Christian, young both in years (I was 19) and in the faith. Having not been raised in any kind of religion, I felt no cultural obligation to the church. It had better make sense, or I didn't need to waste my time. And at this particular moment it wasn't making sense. . .at all.

My challenger was an intelligent man with a point I could not refute. Our visit began with me sharing my new faith with him, but quickly took a hairpin turn that would forever alter my thinking. Right in the middle of my testimony, he broke in:

"Young man," he addressed me with a condescending grin, "why, of all the religions in the world, did you choose Christianity?"

I was eager to answer. With a confidence beyond my knowledge, I swiftly replied, "I'm a Christian because Jesus Christ suffered and died for me. He was whipped, beaten, mocked, crowned with sharp thorns and nailed to a cross. It was terrible, and it was for me. Because of His great sacrifice, I choose to serve Him."

Feeling quite satisfied with my shallow-deep answer, I leaned forward, certain he was nearly moved to tears. I was just about to ask him why he would not want to serve such a wonderful Savior. But before I could make my appeal, he looked at me unflinchingly and spoke words that casually flicked my mind into confusion.

"Listen," he laughed as the retort matter-of-factly rolled out of his mouth, "if all it takes is a willingness to suffer a few hours of physical pain and then to die in order to be a savior, then I could be your savior and you could be mine."

Stunned by the strange logic of his argument, I was just about to offer a solution when he plunged forward with intense blows to my neat little idea.

"Who's to say that Peter didn't suffer just as much as Jesus, or more. He was crucified upside down, wasn't he? Does that make him a savior too? Paul had his head chopped off. That had to hurt, at least for a split second (laughs). Many Christian martyrs were burned at the stake. Fire hurts (more laughs). Who's to say being burned alive isn't more painful than crucifixion?

"Big deal," he mocked, "so Jesus was crucified. Lots of people have suffered lots of pain in this world. And lots of people have died for good causes. How does pain and death equate to savior-hood? People are always dying for other people. Moms have died to save their children. Men have died to save their country in time of war."

Needless to say, I was blown away. Maybe you wouldn't have been, but I was. My whole faith rested on the idea that because Jesus suffered and died for me, He was my Savior. All of a sudden the whole thing seemed common, even trite. I sat there speech-less. But Russell wasn't done. After pausing long enough to let my brain almost settle, he continued on, now introducing his own religion to me. By this time I assumed he must be atheist. Far from it, he was a very committed religious man. Ironically, the idea of a suffering savior, which he had just blasted, he now used to prove his religion superior to mine.

"Jesus gets so much credit for being crucified. I resent it. My master suffered far more (no laughing now)."

Near-anger was evident in his voice. I began to sense that someone not human was speaking to me.

Russell proceeded to tell me of a man whom he followed for ten years on "an enlightenment pilgrimage" in India.

"He was the modern incarnation of deity," Russell explained, "the embodiment of truth and love in human form. His words were warmth to my soul. Love, like electrical waves, emanated from his very presence, passing from his body to mine."

Then Russell paused, as if to gain strength to continue on into painful territory.

"One day, after months of threats from his enemies (followers of a rival guru), they came and took him away. With ruthless cruelty, they tied him to a wooden beam and proceeded to slowly tear his flesh from his bones with hot wood-tongs. For prolonged hours they repeatedly heated the tongs in a fire and tore small amounts of flesh from his arms and legs. Gradually they worked inward toward his mid-section, finally tearing at his internal organs."

There were tears forming in his eyes as he told the emotional story of his master's death.

"Finally, my master died in the utter agony imposed by his tormentors."

Then came the punch line.

"As you can see, my master suffered a far more painful death than crucifixion."

What was I to say? Would it be profitable to argue that Jesus suffered more? Think of the futility of such an argument.

"No way! I really think being crucified would be far more painful than having your flesh torn off your bones with red hot wood-tongs."

I've never been crucified, nor have I ever been torn apart with hot iron tongs. Such a debate would be pointless. Russell really believed that his master suffered more than mine. For him, that meant he had the greater savior. It was offensive to him that so much has been made of the crucifixion of Christ while, in his opinion, his master suffered to a greater degree.

As I walked away that day with my religious tail between my legs, my mind was frozen on one nagging question: "Yeah, what is the big deal? So Jesus suffered and died. How does that make Him any more loving or courageous or righteous than other sufferers? Lots of people have suffered and died for others. How does a tortured body equate to salvation for the world?"

To my astonishment, I discovered it doesn't.

To that point in my young Christian life, every sermon I had heard on the cross focused on the physical torture inflicted upon Christ: the severe beating by the Roman soldiers, the crown of thorns, the nails driven through His hands and feet. Every ligament of His body was wrenched as He hung there on the cross struggling to breathe. How cruel and torturous! I felt pity and sympathy for Christ, much the same as Russell felt for his eastern guru. It soon became obvious to me that my fixation on the physical sufferings of Christ had created a blind spot in my theology. I was blind while standing in the light, and I desperately needed to see the deeper meaning of the cross.

My visit with Russell persuaded me that the sufferings of Jesus must somehow differ from all other sufferings, if meaningful at all. For if the sufferings of Christ were of the same nature as those experienced by other human beings, then there is little, if any, saving significance to His crucifixion. Could it be, I began to wonder, that the torture of our Lord's body is merely a window into a deeper suffering that far exceeded the physical pain He endured? Perhaps what wicked men did to His outer person was the lesser part of His agony, a shadowy silhouette of a sacrifice of far greater magnitude. Maybe behind the torn and bleeding flesh of the Son of Man there was an infinite self-sacrifice offered by the Son of God.

In his effort to belittle my faith in Christ, Russell unwittingly opened to my mind a channel of thought which has made me love the Savior all the more.

I'm anxious to share with you what I learned.

I'll be waiting for you in the next chapter.

FATHER: *As I approach the cross of Christ please show me the true significance of His sufferings and death. Open to my feeble intellect the meaning of this mysterious sacrifice. Reveal to my jaded heart the transforming beauty of Your love. May the Holy Spirit illuminate my mind, romance my emotions and grip my will as I focus my longing gaze upon Your Son. I pray in the light of His character. Amen.*

EIGHT
DESTINY: CONSCIOUSNESS

We're all headed for the same place—

with God. Live or die,

full, undimmed encounter

as the case may be.

IN THE BIBLE WE ENCOUNTER the curious idea that there are two kinds of death, not one. Both are the result of sin, but the first is temporary and occurs by purely physical causes, such as disease or tragedy or old age. The second death, however, does not occur on merely a physical level, but rather on the psychological and emotional level. It is an inward death.

The first death, in a sense, is not really death at all. Jesus called it sleep. Consider, for example, the young maiden whom Jesus awakened out of first-death sleep. As He approached the girl's home, after being asked to come and heal her, Jesus said to the mourners, "Weep not; she is not dead, but sleepeth" (Luke 8:52).

Notice Jesus did not merely say the girl was sleeping, but He went a step further and stated, "She is *not* dead." Not understanding His meaning, "they laughed Him to scorn, knowing that she was dead" (Luke 8:53). Jesus was not off in His diagnosis. He knew the girl was dead in the first-death sense. But He also knew she was not dead in the ultimate, second-death sense. In order to demonstrate His point, He proceeded to awaken the girl from her first-death sleep.

Consider also the case of Lazarus. Speaking to His disciples, Jesus said, "Our friend Lazarus sleepeth; but I go, that I may awake him out of sleep. Then said His disciples, Lord, if he sleeps, he shall do well. Howbeit Jesus spake of his death: but they thought that He had spoken of taking of rest in sleep. Then said Jesus unto them plainly, Lazarus is dead" (John 11:11-14).

"Yes, Lazarus is dead," Jesus conceded, but He was reluctant to call it death. He much preferred to call it sleep. It seems that Jesus understood something about death that we humans don't generally grasp.

The maiden "is not dead," Jesus insists.

"Lazarus is just sleeping."

That's not really death, He seems to be saying.

With this background on the first death, we can now move into the biblical concept of the second death. Let's begin with a straightforward statement by Jesus:

"Fear not them which kill the body, but are not able to kill the soul: but rather fear Him which is able to destroy both soul and body in hell" (Matthew 10:28).

Here Jesus presents two distinct kinds of death. The first is merely the killing of the body. That's all. But the second death is utter destruction, encompassing both body and soul.

I realize the Bible elsewhere uses the word *soul* to mean the whole person: body, mind, emotions, etc. But here Jesus clearly uses the word as distinct, although not separate, from the body. He says the second death is the destruction of *both* (two things) the soul and the body. In this usage, the body is obviously the physical matter that composes our flesh. The soul is the inner person and all that includes—the individual identity, personality, character, mind and emotions. This is what Paul calls "the inner man" (Ephesians 3:16). There is no consciousness of the soul apart from the body, but there is, nevertheless, an inner dimension to human nature that survives the death of the body in the first death, but is utterly destroyed in the second death.

The Bible clearly says that when a person dies the first death, "The dust [flesh] will return to the earth as it was, and the spirit will return to God who gave it" (Ecclesiastes 12:7, NKJV). In other words, the body decomposes in the earth and the *inner man*, the distinct life or identity of the individual, returns to God who gave it. The spirit does not exist with God on any kind of conscious level in the first death, but it is clearly preserved by the Creator for future resurrection. God remembers or maintains a record of the unique personality or character of each person who dies the first death. Therefore, in the resurrection, we will be exactly the same individuals we were before passing into the unconsciousness of first-death sleep.

What, then, is the second death? Jesus said the second death is the destruction of both the body and the soul. In other words, the second death is of an internal nature, in which there is no preservation of character or personality, and from which there is no hope of resurrection. It is a soul-level death, otherwise known in Scripture as the full "wages of sin" (Romans 6:23).

In the end-time book of Revelation, we encounter the second death with chilling, vivid clarity. Chapter twenty describes the destiny of the saved as well as the final demise of those who have chosen to reject the salvation of Christ. Of the saved it says, "On such the second death hath no power" (Revelation 20:6). They escape the second death for good reason: they have embraced Christ as their deliverer, which indicates that He must have endured that death for all the world. But now I'm getting ahead of myself. Moving on in Revelation twenty, the lost are brought to view.

As the wicked surround the New Jerusalem, John says, "Fire came down from God out of heaven and devoured them" (Revelation 20:9). However, the fire from heaven is not the whole picture of the second death. So the prophet backs up to give a more detailed description of what will take place before fire devours the wicked. Remember at this point that the second death is not merely a death of the body. Rather, it encompasses both body and soul. The literal fire that consumes flesh and bone is the lesser part of the second death. It is, in fact, a merciful conclusion to the second death.

Notice what John says as he describes the second death:

"Then I saw a great white throne and Him who sat on it, from whose face the earth and the heaven fled away. And there was found no place for them. And I saw the dead, small and great, standing before God, and books were opened. And another book was opened, which is the Book of Life. And the dead were judged according to their works, by the things which were written in the books" (Revelation 20:11, 12, NKJV).

Give careful attention to this passage of Scripture. Here is opened to our understanding the serious reality of the second death. It is more, far more than merely a physical death of the body. In fact, the physical death by literal fire would seem to be a kind of sweet release from the soul anguish inherent in the second death. Revelation 20 brings to view three dimensions of the second death.

1. *Consciousness of God's Righteousness and Love*: The second death is initiated by a full revelation of God Almighty, seated upon "a great white throne" with His "face" fully exposed to the astonished gaze of all. Paul calls this event "the day of wrath and *revelation* of the righteous judgment of God" (Romans 2:5). Wrath occurs in the light of "revelation." The revelation proceeds from God and takes on the form of self-realization in those who behold it.

It is inevitable that every created being encounter his Maker. In this sense, the ultimate destiny of each person, both believers and unbelievers, is exactly the same. We are all bound for a full, unveiled encounter with God. All will stand before His throne and see His face. All will not, however, see the same dimension of reality in that face. The divine countenance will be the same toward all, but all will not behold the same thing as they look upon it. All will not think the same thoughts and feel the same feelings as they meet the undimmed reality of God's character.

Those who have trusted in Jesus as the true image of God will see infinite love and mercy in the face of God. They will sense the accepting embrace of His unalterable love. But the wicked, both of heaven and earth, fallen angels as well as men, will be compelled from within their sin-damaged souls to flee away from such a God as this. They will feel within themselves an irrepressible impulse to run and hide, not because the divine face flashes with hostility, but because it shines brilliant with a love they cannot bear. It is unbearable from their own twisted perspective, not unbearable due to any change of character on God's part.

Unbearable because they have rejected that beckoning love over and over again.

Unbearable because the infinite contrast between God's changeless love and their own selfishness is more than they can tolerate.

Unbearable because they have formed within themselves a character so contrary, thoughts and feelings so opposite, that the love of their Creator appears as condemnation to them.

They cannot see Him any other way. Their sin-darkened hearts are forever blinded to the beauty of the divine character. Psychologically and emotionally they are left with only the capacity for condemnation. Everything in them is urgent to flee away from the One who was so good to them while they hated Him. The guilty conscience cannot endure the presence of the One who gave His life for them while they lived for themselves. Eternal love itself, by its very nature, is utter condemnation to sin and selfishness. It is by *contrast*, not by *sameness*, that God's righteousness is destructive to sin.

While God does not condemn the sinner, His righteousness and love does condemn sin. Those who ultimately identify themselves with sin so intimately that they cannot separate from it will perish in its condemnation. God will not destroy unrepentant sinners by assuming toward them an unrighteous attitude contrary to love, but rather by maintaining the glorious integrity of His love without wavering. The revelation of God's perfect righteousness and love will destroy the wicked.

2. *Consciousness of Separation*: "There was found no place for them" (Revelation 20:11). These are some of the most horrifying words in all human language. The second death is total aloneness, a deep inner sense of complete unbelonging. The wicked, standing before God's throne and gazing upon His countenance, realize with intense vividness that they are so out of harmony with the universe that there is absolutely "no place for them."

They don't fit into a universe governed by the absolute rule of selfless love. They cannot exist among or interact with a society of beings who live wholly for others. They can't even comprehend such a society. The beautiful ebb and flow of *give-and-receive-with-no-intent-to-get* is beyond their ability to appreciate or engage in. Sin has hollowed their hearts of the capacity for love. Rebellion has stripped away the gentle emotional impulses of the soul. Selfishness has eradicated their sensitive humanity.

The second death confronts the wicked with the bleak reality of an ultimate meaninglessness, for there is no meaning to life apart from its Author. Complete loneliness is all they can feel, for there is no satisfying relationship apart from the One to whom we are most closely related. A sense of total worthlessness pervades their souls, for there can never be any real sense of personal worth apart from an inner reflection of the God who created our value in His own image.

Living for self ultimately leads to self-hatred. Selfishness is, by its very nature, isolation from all others, stealing from the soul the perceptions and emotions necessary to give and receive love. In a universe whose essential life-sustaining principle is selfless love, "there is found no place for them." They sink with regretful self-disgust into acute feelings of total abandonment.

3. *Consciousness of Sin*: "Books were opened. . .and the dead were judged according to their works, by the things which were written in the books" (Revelation 20:12, NKJV).

The second death brings the soul face-to-face with the full, ugly reality of one's sin, untempered by any sense of divine mercy. Sin, once committed, is an existing reality in the mind. It is on record in the conscience and must be resolved either by forgiveness or by suffering. Forgiveness is possible only by means of embracing God's merciful love. Suffering is the only alternative to forgiveness, which is why God can only forgive by means of enduring in Himself the suffering inherent in sin.

The weight of sin's terrible condemnation crushes out the vital life forces of the soul. All human beings are sinners. Therefore, all are under condemnation. That condemnation will eventually, ultimately impose an unbearable shame upon those whose minds refuse to see the healing reality of God's pardoning love. A conscious sense of God's love and acceptance is the only power capable of neutralizing the power of sin and preventing it from destroying the soul.

In order to grasp what the Bible means when it says, "the books were opened…and the dead were judged," try to imagine the unimaginable. Try to imagine what it would be like if you were made perfectly conscious of every sin you've ever committed—every wrong thought and feeling and action; perfect awareness, all at once, with every ugly detail staring at your inner soul with no way of escape. Then add to that horrendous picture an absolute absence of mercy—no concept of forgiveness; no sense of acceptance; no picture of a God who freely and eagerly pardons all sin.

What would that moment in time be like for you? I know what it would be like for me. There are no words adequate to describe the mind-shattering ordeal. Such is the nature of that death which is the full wages paid by sin. The only reason we have never had to face the full potency of our guilt is because the plan of salvation, set into motion by a loving Creator, has erected a veil of mercy in the human conscience to act as a buffer to preserve us from sin's full effect. He has held at bay our suffering by forgiving us at the expense of His own suffering in Christ Jesus.

Revelation 20 pictures the wicked gathered around God's throne. They are *judged* or made conscious by *the books* which have chronicled every sin they have ever committed. By some divinely chosen method, perhaps a great video-screen-like panorama stretching across the sky, every hardened rebel will see the part he or she has played in the great war between good and evil. Every deed of their lives will be etched with vivid clarity upon their mind's eye as with letters of fire. The blazing light of infinite love will clash in their souls with the dark ugliness of sin. The striking contrast will burn with an internal fire hotter and more terrible than any literal flame upon the flesh.

Now comes the vital question, fraught with mind-bending implications: which death, first or second, did Jesus suffer in order to save the human race? Hurry into the next chapter before our backdrop becomes hazy in your mind.

DEAR LORD: *What did Jesus endure on my behalf? Did He really experience the full wages of my sin, and that of the whole human race? Please enter my mind and help me to understand the truth regarding this matter. I want to see the complete measure of Your love as it was manifested in the sacrifice of Your Son. Give me more than human understanding. I pray in view of Jesus Christ. Amen.*

NINE
LOVE BEYOND KNOWLEDGE

When the darkness was the absolute

in sight . . . He chose

darkest . . . no life beyond the grave

our eternal life over His own.

I'D LIKE TO INVITE YOU to engage with me in a spiritual experiment. The hypothesis of the experiment is that God's love is more powerful than sin, that the love of God as revealed in the cross of Christ, when seen and believed, naturally turns the heart away from sin.

Your part is quite simple. But if all goes according to plan, the whole thing will not end up simple at all. To the contrary, the experiment promises to yield some very satisfying results; and, I might add, some incredibly powerful results.

All you have to do is pay attention to what happens in your heart and mind as we go through this chapter. Take note of your thoughts and feelings. Especially be aware of any activity occurring in your will, such as a strong sense of desire or determination.

Ready? Let's begin.

As Jesus and His disciples approach the Garden of Gethsemane, something extremely significant is about to happen. In fact, all of history is about to converge at a single point of destiny, toward which each day and every event have been relentlessly rushing. Just now, in the next relatively brief period of time, the crescendo of all divine self-disclosure, the apex of infinite love, will burst into the visible, tangible dimension of reality. And the world, indeed the universe, will never again be the same.

Watch.

"Then Jesus came with them [His disciples] to a place called Gethsemane, and said to the disciples, 'Sit here while I go and pray over there.' And He took with Him Peter and the two sons of Zebedee, and He began to be sorrowful and deeply distressed. Then He said to them, 'My soul is exceedingly sorrowful, even to death'" (Matthew 26:36-38, NKJV).

Strange, don't you think?

Jesus has not yet been taken to Calvary, and yet He is dying. No one has laid a hand on His physical person. He has not been betrayed. No crown of thorns has been pressed upon His brow. No nails have been hammered through His flesh. Nor has He even been beaten by Pilate's ruthless soldiers.

And yet, right here, right now, in the quietude of a midnight-serene garden, the Savior tells His disciples that He is on the verge of death.

On second thought, it's not strange at all. Did you notice that the Savior's words pointed to His *soul* as the point at which this mysterious death is occurring? And did you notice He said the cause of His dying is a *sorrow* so intense that it's lethal? "My soul (not His body) is exceedingly sorrowful, even to death."

This is no kind of dying from physical causes. Jesus is experiencing a soul-level death. Something that exceeds sorrow is preying upon His inner person. It seems as though sorrow is the best word He can find to describe what He's going through, and yet, the word falls short. So He says, *What I'm experiencing is beyond sorrow. It's an internal pain so great, so deep, so intense that it's stealing My life away.*

He had earlier told His disciples, "Do not fear those who kill the body but cannot kill the soul. But rather fear Him who is able to destroy both soul and body in hell" (Matthew 10:28, NKJV). On the one hand, there is such a thing as mere physical death. On the other hand, there is the death of both the body and the soul. By His own description, Jesus is obviously entering the dark realm of the second death, the one that involves the soul. But what exactly is it, and what does it mean for the Savior?

The prophet Isaiah foretold the sacrifice of Christ and made repeated mention that the Savior would suffer and die at the soul level of His being. Isaiah gives a graphic description of the awful ordeal, which clearly opens to us the nature of our Lord's sacrifice. Notice the inspired words carefully:

"He is despised and rejected by men, a Man of sorrows and acquainted with grief. . .Surely He has borne our griefs and carried our sorrows; yet we esteemed Him stricken, smitten by God, and afflicted. But He was wounded for our transgressions, He was bruised for our iniquities. . .and the Lord [the Father] has laid on Him [the Son] the iniquity of us all. . .For the transgressions of My people He was stricken. . . .His soul [was] an offering for sin. . .He shall see [experience] the labor of His soul, and be satisfied. By His knowledge My righteous Servant shall justify many, for He shall bear their iniquities. . .Because He poured out His soul unto death, and He was numbered with the transgressors, and He bore the sin of many, and made intercession for the transgressors" (Isaiah 53, NKJV, selected verses).

This is an amazing messianic prophecy. It offers incredibly vivid insights into the true nature of Christ's death. Two points stand out:

1. As the premiere Old Testament prophecy of the Savior's sacrifice, Isaiah fifty-three makes little if any mention of physical suffering. Rather, Isaiah describes a deeper agony that would occur on the internal, emotional level. Three times he says the Savior's suffering and death would center in His "soul."

2. The lethal ingredients of His death would be grief, sorrow and sin. This explains why His suffering was primarily internal. Sin produces the excruciating psychological and emotional phenomenon the Bible calls *condemnation* or *guilt*. Jesus did not merely experience the sense of condemnation attached to one person's life of sin, but rather, "the iniquity of us all." In His own heart and mind He was plunged into the collective whole of all human evil as though He were the guilty party. He took into Himself, as the responsible One, the mental and emotional horror that sin's condemnation ultimately imposes on the inner consciousness of the soul.

With Isaiah's added insight as a backdrop, let us return to the Garden of Gethsemane.

After telling His disciples He is dying a soul level death, He "fell on His face, and prayed, saying, 'O My Father, if it be possible, let this cup pass from Me; nevertheless, not as I will, but as Thou wilt'" (Matthew 26:39). This agonizing prayer, pouring forth from the Savior's heart, opens our understanding to the nature of His pain and the cause of His death. So great is His anguish that He actually ventures to ask for relief, but only "if it is possible." Do you discern the conflict in His heart, and do you see yourself at the center of that conflict? He is pleading, *If it is possible to save fallen humanity by any other means, then let Me forgo drinking this cup; but if they can be saved only in this way, even this I am willing to endure for them. I love them even more than My own life.*

Jesus is here facing a death that involves no nails or crown of thorns, but rather a "cup." The symbolic cup, which He holds to His quivering lips, explains the mystery of His soul agony. With perhaps the most frightening language in all of Scripture, the apostle John defines the cup. It is "the wine of the wrath of God, which is poured out without mixture into the cup of His indignation" (Revelation 14:10). In the Garden of Gethsemane Jesus is beginning to experience the wrath of God "without mixture," meaning full strength, undiluted justice without a single tinge of mercy added to water down the force of its potency. He is entering the dark realm of that "death" which is "the wages of sin" (Romans 6:23). Tremblingly, He ventures into the mental and emotional suffering which is inherent in wrongdoing, and which no human being has ever had to face on his own account due to the shielding mercy of God. Acute consciousness of the bridgeless chasm that exists between God's love-infused righteousness and mankind's self-absorbed sinfulness intensifies within Him. And— horror of all horrors—He senses in His inmost soul that He is moving over to the wrong side of the chasm by taking our sin into Himself. "He [God the Father] hath made Him [God the Son] to be sin for us, who knew no sin; that we might be made the righteousness of God in Him" (2 Corinthians 5:21).

On our behalf, He alone is the guilty One. He is bowed down under the condemnation of every evil motive and deed, every hateful feeling, every ugly thought, every rape and murder, every act of child abuse, every war and holocaust, every sin of every person who has ever or will ever live. In His conscience He feels the tormenting blows of shame and self-abhorrence that sin imposes on the soul as its ultimate exaction. Prostrate upon His face, the Son of God is enveloped in the impenetrable darkness of our rebellion. Hopeful thoughts of His resurrection, of which He has previously spoken with such confidence, begin to fade from view, receding to the other side of the darkness. Yet, He does not relent, although He would later tell Peter that He could, at any time, call more than twelve legions of angels to His rescue (see Matthew 26:53). His back is not against a wall. His soul is not held to the flame by a forceful hand beyond His control. He is free to love or to hate, to embrace or to abandon. And that freedom to choose puts His love to the ultimate test.

As Messiah struggles and prays, reaching upward to His Father and downward to fallen humanity, there is an unspoken question that hangs heavy in the atmosphere: "Does God love others more than Himself? When faced with the ultimate decision to preserve self at the loss of others or to save others at the loss of self, what will the divine One choose?"

Jesus is the answer. He is at liberty to abandon humanity to eternal destruction in order to keep His own life, or He may lay hold of our salvation at the expense of His own life. The good news of the gospel here emerges in all its healing beauty, for the strength of His love leaves Him with one prevailing passion. No matter where this path of suffering leads, He cannot leave us to perish. His decision is made: He will save mankind at any cost to Himself. He cannot do otherwise, for the essence of His character is selfless love.

Luke's gospel informs us that God did send an angel to Christ in His Gethsemane agony, not to deliver, however, but to strengthen Him to drink the cup of suffering even to its bitter dregs (see Luke 22:43). The implication is clear: Jesus would have died in the Garden and never reached Calvary had not the angel intervened with words of encouragement. The most intense suffering was yet to come. As the mob approached, led by Judas the betrayer, Christ aroused with regained composure, knowing that the darkest hours of His sacrifice, and the brightest revelation of His love, were just ahead.

"And when they were come to the place, which is called Calvary, there they crucified Him" (Luke 23:33).

The Gospels record no word of complaint from Christ, not even an agonizing cry, as they drove the nails through His hands and feet. In my early understanding of the cross, I assumed that this was a demonstration of great self-control on His part. Actually it was not self-control that held His tongue as they tortured His body. Rather, it was the reality of a lesser pain eclipsed by a greater. What they were doing to His body was nothing compared to what He was going through in His heart and mind. The physical pain was horrible, no doubt. But it was superceded by the soul agony He felt as He became guilty before God of all human iniquity.

Upon the cross, bearing the weight of the sin of the whole world, the Savior cries out from His inmost soul, "My God, My God, why hast Thou forsaken Me?" (Matthew 27:46). Here is the real sacrifice. Here is the true suffering of the Son of God. Here is the death from which He had sought release in the garden, and yet willingly walked into for our eternal salvation. Here is the crescendo revelation of divine love. "My God, My God, why have You forsaken Me?"

Hanging between heaven and earth, Jesus feels, with acute sensitivity, the separation that sin will ultimately make between God and unrepentant sinners. He alone bears it. No one else, not one person in all of history, has ever experienced the full wages of sin. All divine justice has always been mixed with mercy. But now, the eternal Son of the Father endures the horrific trauma of complete separation from the One who has been His beloved Companion from eternity past. The feelings of guilt are so consuming, the condemnation so dark and so completely pervasive, that He feels utterly "forsaken," forever abandoned and rejected by the Father. No hopeful thoughts of resurrection morning are seen through the encompassing guilt. He cannot see through the darkness to the other side of the tomb. All He can feel is the heart-shattering condemnation of sin.

Psalm eighty-eight is a remarkable prophecy of the suffering, dying Savior. With disquieting clarity it peers into the internal workings of the mind and emotions of Christ as He hung upon the cross. Take a deep breath and read:

"O Lord, God of My salvation, I have cried out day and night before You [are you hearing me?]. Let My prayer come before You; incline Your ear to my cry [are You there?]. For My soul is full of troubles, and My life draws near to the grave. I am counted with those who go down to the pit; I am like a man who has no strength [the stress of this experience is draining Me of all energy], adrift among the dead, like the slain who lie in the grave, whom You remember no more [a death from which there is no apparent return], and who are cut off [eternally separated] from Your [sustaining] hand. You have laid Me in the lowest pit, in darkness, in the depths. Your wrath lies heavy upon Me, and You have afflicted Me with all Your waves [Your abandonment and rejection are pounding upon My soul like the waves of a raging ocean]. . . . I am shut up [confined in this soul darkness], and I cannot get out [I cannot see any way of resurrection from this oblivion into which I sink]. . . . Shall the dead arise and praise You [will there be a resurrection from the death I'm dying]?. . . [from] the place of destruction?. . . Lord, why do You cast off [abandon] My soul [My very life]?. . . I suffer Your terrors. I am distraught. Your fierce wrath has gone over Me; Your terrors have cut Me off" (Psalm 88, NKJV; selected verses).

The forsakenness Christ felt on the cross is here graphically portrayed so that we might know the cost of our redemption. It is evident from this messianic passage that Jesus entered a period of severe testing, during which the true character of His love would be proven or conquered. Enveloped within the impenetrable darkness of our guilt, He could not see beyond His death to the other side of the tomb—"I am shut up, and I cannot get out." Crushed under the weight of our sin, the bright hope of resurrection morning eluded His grasp. Faced with the bleak prospect of eternal separation from His Father, still He did not shrink back. He made the conscious choice to value our eternal life more than His own. If it meant that He would never again enjoy the pleasure of His Father's presence, so be it. Even that fate He would be willing to endure for our salvation.

The agonizing cry of Jesus, "My God, My God, why have You forsaken Me?" is just one sentence from a more detailed prophecy of His struggle. Psalm twenty-two traces the suffering Messiah's internal conflict through to its victorious conclusion. While He entered into the jaws of hopeless despair, benighted by the darkness of complete separation from God, His undying love emerged triumphant by faith in His Father's good character.

Follow as His mind convulses back and forth between despair and faith:

Despair: "My God, My God, why hast Thou forsaken Me? Why art Thou so far from helping Me. . . .I cry. . .but Thou hearest not."

Faith: "But Thou art holy. . . .Our fathers trusted in Thee: they trusted, and Thou didst deliver them. They cried unto Thee, and were delivered: they trusted in Thee, and were not confounded."

Despair: "But I am a worm, and no man; a reproach of men, and despised of the people. . .They shake the head, saying, He trusted on the Lord that He would deliver Him: let Him deliver Him, seeing He delighted."

Faith: "But Thou art He that took Me out of the womb: Thou didst make Me hope when I was upon My mother's breasts. I was cast upon Thee from the womb: Thou art My God from My mother's belly. Be not far from Me; for trouble is near; for there is none to help."

Despair: "I am poured out like water, and all My bones are out of joint; My heart is like wax; it is melted in the midst of My bowels. My strength is dried up. . .Thou hast brought Me to the dust of death. . . . The wicked have enclosed Me: they pierced My hands and feet. . . . They part My garments among them, and cast lots upon My vesture."

Faith: "But be not Thou far from Me, O Lord: O My strength, haste Thee to help Me. Deliver My soul. . . . Save Me from the lion's mouth."

At this point in the Savior's struggle, faith gains the ascendancy and triumphs over despair. The feelings of God-forsakenness are strong, but He is fully resolved to save fallen mankind at any cost to Himself and trust His own future to the Father.

Triumphant Faith: "I will declare Thy name [character] unto My brethren. . . . Ye that fear the Lord, praise Him. . .glorify Him. . . . For He hath not despised nor abhorred the affliction of the afflicted; neither hath He [the Father] hid His face from Him [the Son]; but when He cried unto Him, He heard. . . . Your heart shall live forever. . . . None can keep alive His own soul" (Psalm 22).

Even when faced with the terrifying possibility of an eternal, God-forsaken death, knowing that He could abandon fallen man and save Himself at any moment, the Son of God continued to trudge forward into the darkness with self-forgetful determination. The devastating prospect of never-ending separation from His Father did not alter His decision to ransom the rebellious children whom He loved more than His own soul. Once the trial was borne through to its zenith—where the highest love and the deepest selfishness stood face to face and love gained the victory—then the assurance of the Father's acceptance again encircled His beloved Son. In the trusting sigh, "Father, into Thy hands do I commend My spirit," we catch the glimmers of a victorious faith in the goodness of God. "My God, My God, why hast Thou forsaken Me?" gave way to "He hath not despised nor abhorred [Me as I felt]. . .neither hath He hid His face. . . [My] heart shall [after all] live forever."

"This is love: not that we loved God, but that He loved us and sent His Son as an atoning sacrifice for our sins" (1 John 4:10, NIV).

At the cross of Christ we stand as breathless spectators witnessing the self-forgetful majesty of a love that is beyond our comprehension. So deep, so strong, so utterly selfless and unlike ourselves is this love that we are tempted to deny its existence.

But if we will believe and not deny, its existence will be proved by the influence it will exert over our hard, selfish hearts. By believing that the Christ of Calvary is, in truth, the revelation of the Father's character, sin loses its power over us. Our guilty hearts are bathed in the healing light that streams forth from the Cross, awakening within us a reciprocal love of like character. For it is truly "an atoning sacrifice," making our hearts one with His.

Tears swell in my eyes and adoration surges in my heart as the true significance of the Savior's sacrifice dawns within me. How could He love me so deeply, so passionately, so selflessly? Is this really what God is like? Can it truly be that the Almighty is so incredibly beautiful? Calvary answers with a resounding *Yes!*

Our experiment is now complete. Assess your thoughts and feelings in the glorious light of God's love. How do you feel toward sin? What are your thoughts about God? Do you sense in your heart the awakening of an indomitable power to love and serve such a Lord? Do you feel the arousal of adoration and reverence? Do you find yourself stunned, perhaps even pained, by the radical beauty of God's character?

If so, then say *Yes* to the revelation. Say *Amen* to the love of your Maker. Say *Yes, I do believe that God is truly as good as the cross of Christ says He is.*

How absolutely amazing, Father! *What a heartbreaking wonder it is that Jesus willingly faced the darkness of eternal death, knowing He could save Himself at any moment, and yet He valued my eternal life more than His own. I can hardly believe it. I can hardly bear it. The reality is more than I can grasp or fully appreciate. Truly this is love that passes knowledge. I am driven to my knees and poured out like water at Your feet. In the light of this kind of love I am so weak and yet so strong. By the charming force of the cross, break the power of sin over my heart and teach me how to love like You do. With Your love before me in Christ I pray. Amen.*

TEN

LIFE IN LOVE

$$7 \times 3 - 1 = 0 \times 1 = 7$$

$$1 \times 1 - 0 = 1 \times 0 = 0$$

MYSTERY OF ALL MYSTERIES!

God became a human being in the person of the man Christ Jesus. "History is filled with men who would be God, but only one God who would be man."

The reason He did it is perhaps more marvelous than the fact itself.

"We see Jesus, who was made a little lower than the angels *for* the suffering of death. . .*that* He by the grace of God should taste death for every man. . . . As the children are partakers of flesh and blood, He also Himself likewise took part of the same; *that* through death He might destroy him that had the power of death, that is, the devil" (Hebrews 2:9, 14).

The Creator became the created so He could experience death for every member of the fallen race. The incarnate Son of God received in Himself the full wages paid by sin, which is the inward death of guilt which separates the soul from God (see Romans 6:23). A little logic persuades us that Christ must have tasted the very death from which He saves us. He could not have merely experienced the first death, for it is not merely the first death from which we need redeeming. Without the Savior's intervention, sin would plunge us into the shame-filled darkness of the second death. It follows that it is this very thing which He Himself endured on our behalf.

But right here we encounter another mystery. What about His resurrection? If Jesus did, in actual fact, experience the full wages of sin, why is He not still held in the cruel clutches of that eternal night? Does not His resurrection prove that He somehow bypassed the full measure of our rightful demise?

The answer given by Scripture is enormous in its implications. It is simply, profoundly this: In the death of Christ, death itself was destroyed. His resurrection occurred, not by arbitrary authority, but by actual conquest over death in His submission to it.

After His resurrection, Jesus declared, "I am He that liveth, and was dead; and, behold, I am alive for evermore, Amen; and have the keys of hell and of death" (Revelation 1:18).

"Through death" He has ensured the destruction of "him that had the power of death, that is, the devil" (Hebrews 2:14). He "hath abolished death, and hath brought life and immortality to light through the gospel" (2 Timothy 1:10).

There was something about the Savior's death that fully triumphed over "the power of death." But what was it? How, and by what power, was He raised to life?

In order to understand the victory over death achieved by the Cross, we need first to understand that there are two opposing principles presently operable in the universe: (1) "the law of the spirit of life in Christ Jesus" and (2) "the law of sin and death" (Romans 8:2). In Christ we encounter the operation of the law of life; that is, the fixed principle out of which life naturally flows. Sin, on the other hand, is the fixed law that causes death.

To further clarify his meaning, Paul goes on to explain: "To be carnally minded *is* death; but to be spiritually minded *is* life and peace" (Romans 8:6). Paul is concerned here with two different kinds of minds, leading to two entirely different destinies. One way of thinking and feeling generates death; the other generates life. Then the apostle helps us understand why this is so: "*Because* the carnal mind is enmity against God: for it is not subject to the law of God, neither indeed can be. . . . But the spirit is life *because* of righteousness" (Romans 8:7, 10). Or as Solomon put it, "As righteousness tendeth to life: so he that pursueth evil pursueth it to his own death" (Proverbs 11:19).

Carnal mindedness is here defined as enmity toward God and His law. Sin is a condition of mind that is characterized by rebellion against the principle of life which is present in God's character and expressed in His law. Spiritual mindedness, on the other hand, is a mental and emotional condition which is distinguished by harmony with God's character and law.

What then is the principle of life inherent in God's law? And what is the principle of death present in sin?

God governs the universe by fixed principles, all of which are extensions of a single foundational law. He operates upon the solitary premise of love. He didn't pull the idea out of the air on a whim, as if there could have been another foundation to build upon. Far from it! Love was His only option, because love is His very nature. "God *is* love" (1 John 4:8). It is by virtue of His love that God created life, and it is by the power of His love alone that life is sustained. God's love is the pulsating energy of all life.

By definition, love is other-centeredness; that is, to live for others rather than for self. If we were to define love more specifically, it would read like the Ten Commandment law of God.

This is how to love God:

1. Have no other gods before Him.
2. Do not worship man-made images.
3. Do not take His name upon yourself in vain.
4. Remember to worship Him on the seventh day as a grateful acknowledgement of the fact that He created you and redeemed you by His power alone.

This is how to love other people:

5. Honor your parents.
6. Do not commit murder.
7. Do not commit adultery.
8. Do not steal.
9. Do not lie.
10. Do not be jealous of what others have and wish you could have what belongs to them (see Exodus 20).

God's law is not a list of arbitrary rules concocted by a picky control freak who wants everything to go His way. It is simply the only way to live in harmony with love, and to live in love is the only way to perpetuate life into eternity. Sin is not merely an alternative way of doing things which happens to be contrary to God's opinion. "Sin is transgression of the law" (1 John 3:4). Sin is violation of the life-sustaining principle of love spelled out in God's law. All sin, therefore, is selfishness at root level.

God has a law because there is, in actual fact, a right way of doing things and a wrong way. The right way is right because it sustains life. The wrong way is wrong because it destroys life. There is absolutely no arbitrary element in God's character. Things are the way they are because they are, by very nature, that way, and must be that way in order for life to flourish. Do not hear God saying, "If you sin, I'll kill you; but if you do things My way, I'll let you live." Rather, hear Him speak the true reality of the matter: "If you pursue sin, it will destroy you; but if you turn to Me and embrace My love, that love will restore and sustain you for all eternity."

God's law=love=life.

Sin=selfishness=death.

In order to create a life-sustaining universe, certain concrete principles were built into that life-structure. The law of God, which is the love of God expressed in practical terms, is absolutely indispensable to a universe designed to support everlasting life. It defines the very nature of life and the conditions under which life will continue. God engineered creation to function in harmony with His love. The life we have is the product of His love. "God is love. Whoever lives in love lives in God, and God in him" (1 John 4:16, NIV). What fuel is to an engine; what oxygen is to fire; what electricity is to a lamp; what sunshine is to vegetation, God's love is to life. God's love is the psychological and emotional fuel of our existence. Death is inevitable in the absence of that essential, energizing force. The very design of our inner spiritual being makes us utterly dependent on love. We must see and believe God's love for us; and we must, in turn, pour out that love on Him and on all others in order to experience the health of eternal life.

Sin is the complete antithesis of God's love. As love is other-centeredness, sin is self-centeredness. As love is life, sin is death.

"Sin, when it is finished, bringeth forth death" (James 1:15).

"The soul that sinneth, it shall die" (Ezekiel 18:4).

"The wages of [paid by] sin is death" (Romans 6:23).

"The sting of death is sin" (1 Corinthians 15:56).

"He that sinneth against Me wrongeth his own soul: all they that hate Me love death" (Proverbs 8:36).

Sin not only violates God, it also wrongs the soul of the sinner. All those who hate God love death. They are acting in accordance with a principle that erodes life, whether they realize the fact or not. In every sin is a suicidal element. All sin is destructive action of self against self, as well as rebellion against the Creator. By its very nature sin is the mistress of death. In what sense? In the sense that sin is a psychological derangement that dethrones love and exalts self. By sin the soul is robbed of love as the essential principle of life, and is held captive to the illusion that living for self will preserve self. In reality, self-centeredness is the recipe for self-destruction. Selfless love, on the other hand, is the stuff life is made of. By its very nature love is the catalyst of life.

With this background we are now prepared to contemplate the resurrection of Christ. Again we ask, *How could the Savior have truly entered the jaws of death and yet come forth again into the fullness of eternal life?*

According to Paul, *the law of life* and *the law of sin and death* waged their decisive conflict in the person of Jesus Christ (see Romans 8:2). Having taken upon Himself our "sinful flesh," the apostle further states, Jesus lived a life and died a death that "condemned sin in the flesh" (Romans 8:3). That is to say, He lived a sinless life, uncorrupted by selfishness, in the very human nature in which the principle of sin had always reigned. Sin never owned Him. By virtue of His unrelenting love for sinners and His unbroken trust in the Father, Christ neutralized the power of sin in our very humanity. His resurrection is proof of that victory.

Scripture declares: "God raised Him from the dead, freeing Him from the agony of death, because it was impossible for death to keep its hold on Him" (Acts 2:24, NIV).

Why was it impossible for death to hold Him?

Precisely because sin, which is the power of death, had never taken hold of Him. The Father did not resurrect Christ by arbitrary stealth, but by rightful conquest. It was impossible for death to hold Him because He did not selfishly grasp onto His life in resistance to death. Prompted by the power of selfless love, He laid down His life for the salvation of the world.

"I lay down My life," He explained, "that I might take it again. No man taketh it from Me, but I lay it down of Myself. I have power to lay it down, and I have power to take it again" (John 10:17, 18).

Having abandoned self for the good of others, He triumphed over the principal essence of sin, thereby nullifying its power to destroy Him. The fact that no one took His life against His will proves that it was given voluntarily in love. If men had taken His life against His will, the very resistance of His will would have proven Him incapable of loving others at any cost to Himself. Sin would have prevailed over love. But because He submitted to the complete loss of self, love remained the dominant force in his heart. The words, "I lay down My life, *that* I might take it up again," establish a vital connection between His willing sacrifice and His victorious resurrection. For if sin is the power of death, and if the essence of sin is selfishness, then it follows that the selfless love of Christ, maintained even to the point of death, is the power by which He overcame the law of sin and death.

It was Satan's diabolical purpose to thwart the love of Christ for fallen mankind and to break His trust in the Father. The condemnation of our sin upon Him, the corresponding sense of separation from God, the abuse and cruelty heaped upon Him by those He came to save—all was calculated to wrench love from His heart and force Him into self-centeredness. "The rulers. . .derided Him, saying, He saved others; *let Him save Himself*, if He be the Christ, the chosen of God. . . . The soldiers also mocked Him. . .saying. . .*save Thyself.* . . . And one of the malefactors which were hanged railed on Him, saying, If Thou be Christ, *save Thyself* and us" (Luke 23:35-39).

Save self! Save self! Save self!

Everything about the cross event pressured the Son of God in the direction of self-preservation. The core essence of God's character was under siege. Who is the Ruler of the universe? What is He made of at heart? Will His love prove a sham, or will it plunge to the deepest depths of self-sacrifice?

When taunted by the ugliness of our selfish hatred, will Christ continue to love us with selfless abandon? When confronted with the darkness of complete separation from His Father, will He keep on putting us first? As the Savior hung in soul-torture upon the tree, despised by men and apparently forsaken by God, love and selfishness stood face to face in raging combat. In Christ, the principle of sin-equals-death measured strength against the law of love-equals-life, and love gained the victory. Calvary placed on record for all eternity the vindicating reality that God is infinitely, intrinsically selfless. All intelligent worship and all true loyalty are forever His by virtue of the cross. And all rebellion against such a God is proven futile and unjustifiable.

Pondering the meaning of the Cross, Jesus said to the disciples, "He that loveth his life shall lose it; and he that hateth his life in this world shall keep it unto life eternal. . . . For this cause came I unto this hour. . . now shall the prince of this world be cast out. And I, if I be lifted up from the earth [on the cross], will draw all unto Me" (John 12:25, 27, 31, 32).

The death and resurrection of Christ constituted the death knell for Satan's kingdom. "Having disarmed the powers and authorities [of darkness], He made a public spectacle of them, triumphing over them by the cross" (Colossians 2:15, NIV). Calvary disarmed the devil, securing the ruin of the one who had the power of death. All the intelligent beings of the universe are drawn to the Son of God in settled loyalty due to the self-sacrificing love manifested in His life and death. In Christ, the true science of life is demonstrated. "Whosoever exalteth himself shall be abased; and he that humbleth himself shall be exalted" (Luke 14:11). The way to up is down, and the way to down is up. To live for self is to destroy one's relationships with all others and lose their trust. To live for others is the way of life. Through apparent defeat, Christ is victorious. All who see clearly are drawn to Him while Satan is *cast out*. Through self-exaltation the fallen angel's influence is forever shattered.

The triumph of the Cross is the triumph of love. Coming forth from the grave, Christ won the war against sin and death. And His conquest is ours. Plan on living forever, if you plan on living in His love.

GRACIOUS GOD: *What a wonder You are. Truly You are great in wisdom. You are mighty through weakness. You are exalted through humility. You are alive through death. I'm convinced that the way of life is the way of self-sacrificing love. Teach me and empower me to live in that way. I am so frail, so prone to lift myself up and pull others down. Break me free. Cause me to walk at liberty. May I soar in your love. In the light of Christ, I pray. Amen.*

ELEVEN
TIMELESS CALVARY

The collective whole of all human reality. He is the Almighty, and yet He

in all the universe.

suffering is His constant, conscious

is the most sensitive person

STANDING IN AWE at the foot of the cross, we can't help but sense we are peering into a reality which transcends *that time* in AD 31 and *that space* on a hill far away. The beautiful-ugly spectacle before our eyes reaches into us and speaks of something more, something larger, than a single event of history. We are face to face with the *eternal* heart of God.

What occurred at Calvary was *revelation*, not *creation*—a revelation of something that already was, not a creation of something that had no prior existence. God was not appeased by the blood of Christ to love with a love newly aroused by the sacrifice. He was not prompted by the sufferings of Jesus to forgive with a forgiveness previously unknown to Him. The Cross rather unfolded the timeless identity of the Almighty. In the historical event of Calvary, God said, in essence, *This is who I am, who I always have been and who I always will be. I am a God of humble self-denial for the precious others I have made. I am a God of infinite, self-sacrificing love. Behold Me! This. . .yes, this that is before you on the cross. . .is who I am.*

Prior to the event of the Cross, its principal essence was already a reality for God. As soon as sin arose in Eden, there was an active, affected Savior. Immediately, the heart of God began to bear the pain of our rebellion and cover our transgression with the preserving power of His forgiveness. Likewise, once Jesus died and rose again, that suffering did not cease. Calvary merely, gloriously, lifted the curtain, as it were, to bring into open view the agony that had been alive in the divine heart all along. As the Son of God was taken down from the cross and buried, the curtain was once more closed to hide from our eyes a suffering that yet continues. Jesus is "the Lamb slain from the foundation of the world" (Revelation 13:8). And with every sin men and women commit, "they crucify to themselves the Son of God afresh, and put Him to an open shame" (Hebrews 6:6).

One day it dawned on me that because "God created man in His own image" (Genesis 1:27), not only is man like God, but the reverse is also true: God is like man. Of course, He is not like us in every way. There are many ways in which He is completely unlike us. He is God. We are not. But the ways in which He is unlike us do not negate the fact that He did make us like Himself in some certain other ways. And if we are like Him, then He is like us. So understanding ourselves can be helpful in understanding what He is like.

I am a physical person. I have a body. Does God have a body? Is He, if and when He chooses to be, a physical person? The Bible seems to say *yes*. The apostle John promised that we "shall see His face" (Revelation 22:4). God has a face, and one day we will see it. That face has eyes according to Scripture: "The eyes of the Lord are upon the righteous, and His ears are open unto their cry" (Psalm 34:15). God has eyes, and one day we will have the privilege of eye contact with the Almighty. On a certain occasion, Moses asked to see God. The Lord answered, "I will take away mine hand, and thou shalt see my back parts: but my face shall not be seen" (Exodus 33:23). God has a backside, which means He must also have a front side. God has a body. We should not be surprised, for "God created man in His own image." This is not to say that God is confined to a body. Jesus once said, "God is a Spirit" (John 4:24). But just because He is a spirit doesn't mean He cannot have a body at will. He can and He does.

What about a mind? Does God have an intellect? Of course He does. He thinks and reasons, as do we, albeit far above us (see Isaiah 1:18). To say that God is intelligent would be a gross understatement, and yet, He is intelligent, infinitely so.

Now let's go a step further.

Does God have a heart, an emotional dimension to His divine

nature? Does He shed tears from His eyes? Does He smile with His face? Does He, God Almighty, feel pain? Does He feel elation and joy? Does He ever struggle or grapple in conflict, pain and joy clashing within Him? Is God an emotional being?

Simply, profoundly, yes.

In fact, God is the most sensitive, passionate, emotional person in all the universe, due to one paramount reality: "God is love" (1 John 4:8). And it is the nature of love to feel, as well as to know and choose.

Look at your own human experience. Is it not true that the measure of your love determines your capacity to feel both sorrow and happiness? In other words, the more you love someone, the more you hurt when they hurt, and the more you soar with joy when they are joyous. The strength of your love calibrates the acuteness of your emotional sensitivity.

Now think of God, remembering that He made humanity in His image. Love is the supreme, pulsating energy of His very being. He must be infinitely emotional, deeply sensitive.

Now return to yourself. Think of the person you love most in this world, perhaps a parent or child, a spouse or friend. Try to imagine how you would feel if that person were dying of some slow killing disease, suffering every hour of every day. What would be the activity of your emotions? There is only one way you could feel, if you truly loved that person. While they would suffer physical pain, you would suffer emotional pain. And the only way your pain could cease would be for your loved one's pain to end. Perhaps you don't have to employ your imagination, but rather your memory. You may be one of the many people who have watched a loved one suffer and die under the curse of disease.

I have.

During the long course of eighteen months I watched my beautiful forty-two-year-young mother die of cancer. She shriveled down to seventy-five pounds of skin and bones. The picture still lingers in my mind. I can see her sitting on her bed rocking back and forth, her head between her hands, crying, "It hurts—it hurts so bad. God, please take my life."

I learned much concerning the human heart—that heart made in the image of God's heart—from my mom's suffering. I learned that it was impossible for her to suffer alone. Her pain pierced my own soul. As long as she was in pain, so was I. When you really love someone, their pain becomes your own.

Now move beyond physical pain, as hard as it can be at times, for there is a kind of pain that far exceeds physical suffering. Try to imagine how you would feel if the person you love most in this world were to stop loving you. What if they were to seriously despise you?

"I want nothing to do with you. Leave me alone. Get out of my life."

No words could sting the heart more deeply than these. It would be difficult to imagine any greater agony than to be utterly rejected by someone you love with every fiber of your being. A rebellious child. A broken marriage vow. A betrayal of friendship.

Again, think of God with all this in mind, not failing to recall that He is like us because we are like Him.

God is love. Warm and sensitive pathos vibrates through His heart. He is not emotionally cold or calloused to the slightest degree. He loves every single man, woman and child with an infinitely greater love than you and I feel for the person we love most. Every sorrow and joy that touches every life throbs in Him with soft, impressionable vitality. He is not jaded, but perfectly sensitive to all human need. He is not blind, but completely conscious of each individual experience. He can no more brush us aside than He can cease to be God.

The Bible is filled with imagery that forcibly communicates this rather human side of God. Some of the pictures are so human that we tend to shy away from them. But they are as biblical as the Ten Commandments.

God the Familiar Friend: There are two men of whom the Bible specifically speaks as friends of God (see Exodus 33:11; Isaiah 41:8). It is interesting to note that both Moses and Abraham had a familiar way of relating to their Maker.

On one occasion the Lord informed Moses that He was going to destroy rebellious Israel and start a new nation with Moses. "The Lord said unto Moses. . .thy people, which thou broughtest out of the land of Egypt, have corrupted themselves" (Exodus 32:7).

Then the Lord said something rather unGodlike to Moses, at least in our common perception of God: "Let Me alone, that My wrath may wax hot against them, and that I may consume them: and I will make of thee a great nation" (Exodus 32:10).

It is those first three words that are so fascinating: "Let Me alone." This is God speaking to a man, and He says, "Let Me alone," as though Moses might have the guts to pursue the Lord and persuade Him to change His mind. If God said to you, "I'm going to destroy this people, and don't you try to stop Me," what would you do? Would you leave Him alone? Would you even dare to think you could talk God out of His plan? Moses did.

"Let Me alone," God said. The next verse says, "And Moses besought the Lord his God."

Don't you get it, Moses? God said, *Leave Me alone.*

I know, the old prophet seems to say, *but I'm not going to leave Him alone; I'm going to reason with Him. I think I can calm His passion and persuade Him of a better plan.*

"Lord, why doth Thy wrath wax hot against Thy people, which Thou hast brought forth out of the land of Egypt with great power, and with a mighty hand?" (Exodus 32:11).

What a question!

God, why are you so angry with Your *people?*

God had just disowned them and called them "*thy* people," Moses, "which *thou* broughtest out of the land of Egypt." Now Moses says, *They are* Thy *people that* Thou *hast brought out of Egypt.*

Then Moses tells the Lord that destroying Israel won't be good for His reputation with the Egyptians, and pleads, "turn from Thy fierce wrath, and repent of this evil against Thy people. Remember Abraham, Isaac, and Israel, Thy servants, to whom Thou swarest by Thine own self, and said unto them, I will multiply your seed" (Exodus 32:12, 13).

Does God have a memory problem? Has He forgotten His promise to Abraham, Isaac and Jacob? Does the Almighty need Moses to reason things out with Him? Or do we rather encounter here a very passionate God struggling with His people; and Moses, His close friend, sympathizing with the Lord and helping Him through this tough time?

To think that He had delivered them from Egyptian bondage, cared for them day and night, fed them, guided them, and now they were having an idolatrous orgy around a false Egyptian god made of gold. What complete ingratitude! What total moral decadence! What an incredible lack of love for Him! It was all so agonizing to the heart of this One who longingly desires our friendship. *Moses, it's too much. I feel like destroying them and starting over.* And yet it seems clear that the Lord does not really desire to destroy His rebellious people, but wants them and Moses to understand how serious and painful the situation is from His perspective. So after expressing His passionate pain and listening to Moses plead on their behalf, God concludes that He will do what was in His heart to do all along: *You're right Moses. I need to trudge on, forgive and bear the pain. I'm pleased to see My grace reflected in your heart.*

The next verse says, "And the Lord repented of the evil which He thought to do unto His people" (Exodus 32:14). The whole thing is pretty astounding. The Lord could have easily said, *Listen Moses, I'm God. Don't you dare talk to Me like that. Who do you think you are?* But He didn't. It seems the Lord desires this kind of intimacy with human beings.

Similarly, Abraham was a close friend of God. The incident with Sodom and Gomorrah is very eye opening. First the Lord muses to Himself, "Shall I hide from Abraham that thing which I do?" (Genesis 18:17). Deciding to tell Abraham His plan, the Lord explains that He is going to destroy the wicked twin cities.

"And Abraham drew near, and said, Wilt Thou also destroy the righteous with the wicked. . . . That be far from Thee to do after this manner. . . Shall not the Judge of all the earth do right?" (Genesis 18:23, 25).

Like Moses, Abraham reasons with the Almighty: *God, I know You better than that. You would never destroy the righteous with the wicked. You're just too good, and You always do what is right.*

Then Abraham begins what resembles a dickering process with the Lord. He is reverent, but persistent, with a bottom-line goal in mind. *If there are fifty righteous people in these cities, will You spare them all?*

God agrees: "If I find in Sodom fifty righteous within the city, then I will spare all the place for their sakes" (Genesis 18:26). Then Abraham lowers the number to forty-five and God agrees. Then forty. Thirty. Twenty. Finally ten. Each time the Lord agrees. Even if there are ten righteous people in the cities, He will not destroy. Later in history, speaking to the prophet Isaiah, God referred to "Abraham My friend" (Isaiah 41:8).

This touching account reveals that God feels pain and frustration as a result of His deep love for people. It hurts Him when human beings despise Him and pursue life in such a way as to abuse and destroy one another. Looking down upon the self-degradation, the rape, the child abuse and murder occurring day by day in Sodom, He could take it no longer. In compassion to the abused and in holy anger toward the evil abusers, He purposed to put them all out of their misery. But before doing so He consulted with one of His close friends, a man named Abraham.

God the Compassionate Parent: The Lord likens Himself to a mother in Scripture: "Can a woman forget her sucking child, that she should not have compassion on the son of her womb? Yea, they may forget, yet will I not forget thee. Behold, I have graven thee upon the palms of My hands" (Isaiah 49:15, 16).

Is there any stronger sympathy, any deeper love, than that of a mother for her child? God wants us to make the connection. He can't get us off His mind. Like a mother who cannot forget to feed her baby, so God cannot forget our needs. Day and night He bears us upon His tender, parental heart.

Repeatedly Jesus introduced God to the people as their Father. He taught them to pray, "Our Father which art in heaven. . ."

(Matthew 6:9). He portrayed the Almighty as a "Father" who loves to "give good things to them that ask Him" (Matthew 7:11).

In the story of the prodigal son, He likened God to a father coping with a rebellious teenager. Reluctantly, the Father gives us what we demand, even though He knows, painfully so, that we are headed for lots of disappointment. Eagerly He waits for us to come to our senses, hoping we don't destroy ourselves first. When we do finally realize our horrible crime against Him, He embraces us with tears. Making no mention of our foolishness, He throws an extravagant party to welcome us home (see Luke 15:11-32). This is what God is like, according to Jesus. He longs to hear us cry out to Him from our rebellious teenage hearts, "My Father, Thou art the guide of my youth" (Jeremiah 3:4).

God the Wounded Husband: Jealous. Sensitive. Hurt. Discouraged. Vulnerable. Are these words that naturally come to mind when you think of God?

I didn't think so.

And yet, this is the picture we get by reading the God-as-a-rejected-husband passages of the Old Testament. Over and over again the image is presented: the Lord lavishing faithfulness and blessing on His people as a caring husband, only to be jilted for other lovers. He pleads. He weeps. He rages. He threatens. He forgives. He throws her out, then takes her back again.

"Thou hast played the harlot with many lovers; yet return again to Me, saith the Lord. . . . Surely as a wife treacherously departeth from her husband, so have ye dealt treacherously with Me" (Jeremiah 3:1, 20).

From Scriptures like this we can enter into the feelings of God and understand the meaning of His wrath as expressed throughout the Old Testament. We often misunderstand the wrath of God by viewing it as a kind of heartless hostility as if He were mean and uncaring. But when we see the Almighty expressing Himself as a jilted lover vulnerable to emotional pain, then we are approaching the true picture. He is a God who is far from heartless. To the contrary, He is so very full of heart that He has no choice but to respond to our insensitive abuses.

In order to clearly communicate His predicament with a rebellious and wayward people, God went so far as to have one of His prophets give a living object lesson. Hosea was told to marry a prostitute by the name of Gomer. He was to endure the pain of her unfaithfulness. It was as if the Lord was saying, *Do you feel those feelings, Hosea? They're deep, aren't they? It's painful, isn't it, to love someone so much you can't let them go even in the face of their blatant rejection?*

Take in the intense emotions of God as He describes His struggles:

"Ye are not My people, and I will not be your God...

"I will not have mercy. . .

"I will destroy. . .

"For she went after her lovers, and forgot Me, saith the Lord. . .

On second thought:

"I will allure her, and bring her into the wilderness, and speak comfortably to her. . .and it shall be at that day, saith the Lord, that thou shalt call Me Ishi [My husband]. . .

"And I will betroth thee unto Me forever; yea, I will betroth thee unto Me in righteousness, and in judgment, and in lovingkindness, and in mercies. I will even betroth thee unto Me in faithfulness: and thou shalt know the Lord. . . .

"And I will have mercy upon her that had not obtained mercy; and I will say to them which were not My people, thou art My people; and they shall say, Thou art my God."

And yet, He cannot ignore what He sees:

"I have seen an horrible thing in the house of Israel: there is the whoredom of Ephraim, Israel is defiled. . . .

"There is none among them that calleth unto Me. . .

"I will chastise. . .

"They rebel against Me. . .

"Israel hath cast off the thing that is good. . .

"How long will it be ere they attain to innocency? . .

"Ephraim hired lovers. . . .

"Thou hast gone a whoring from thy God. . . .

"It is in My desire that I should chastise them. . . .

"I draw them with cords of a man, with bands of love. . . .

"My people are bent to backsliding from Me."

And yet:

"How shall I give thee up. . .Mine heart is turned within Me, My repentings are kindled together."

Then comes the final resolve:

"I will not execute the fierceness of Mine anger, I will not return and destroy. . .for I am God, and not man [as if He needs to remind Himself]. . .

"O Israel, thou hast destroyed thyself; but in Me is thine help. . .

"For thou hast fallen by thine iniquity. . .

"I will heal their backsliding, I will love them freely; for mine anger is turned away from him" (Selections from Hosea).

Do you sense the passionate conflict between love for His people and hatred for their sin? Can you feel the pulsating, back and forth, almost fickle struggle raging in the divine heart? One moment He rejects, the next He embraces.

"I will destroy," He cries. And then, "I will not destroy."

"I will chastise." No, "I will heal and love freely."

We have tended to make God so distant, so big, so nearly sterile that we have forgotten that He is a person. A person who made us in His image. A person, therefore, who has a heart that feels joy and pain like ours. And His heart is infinitely more sensitive, as His love is infinitely greater than ours. All the passion of the universe has its origin in Him; and therefore all passion, both the pleasurable and painful, finds resonance in Him as well. Every pain that is felt, every sigh that is breathed, every sorrow that pierces the soul, like a rushing current of sympathetic vibration, throbs to the Father's heart.

When we hurt, He hurts. Of Israel's long history of suffering, Isaiah declared, "In all their afflictions, He was afflicted. . . in His love and in His pity He redeemed them; and He bare them, and carried them all the days of old" (Isaiah 63:9). Can you imagine? The God of the universe literally feels the collective whole of all human afflictions! He sees everything that transpires on this reeling planet, every moment of every day. No individual life ever escapes His notice. He sees and feels it all, and His anguish is proportional to His love.

Of Jesus it is written that He is "touched with the feeling of our infirmities" (Hebrews 4:15). What a Savior! "For He that toucheth you," the prophet declares, "toucheth the apple of His eye" (Zechariah 2:8). You have never experienced a sorrow or grief or heartache or shame that did not also encompass Him in its tearful embrace. Christ went so far as to say that whatever we do to any other person, or fail to do, He feels the blow or the blessing as if He were the direct recipient. "Inasmuch as ye have done it unto one of the least of these My brethren, ye have done it unto Me" (Matthew 25:40). When we bring relief, He is relieved. When we inflict injustice, He is wronged. When we help, He is helped. When we impose pain, He is pained.

The cross of Christ has lifted the curtain for a glorious, flashing moment, giving us an interior view of the heart of God. There we encounter the greatest love of all. And there, because of that love, we gaze for an instant into the greatest agony of all: God bearing our sin, not merely for a few hours on an old rugged cross, but from the day Adam and Eve first broke that strong but sensitive heart. . .until this very moment.

Calvary is timeless, perhaps even immortal. Will God ever, even in eternity future, cease to hold back tears for the precious ones who never said *yes* to His saving love?

"And one shall say unto Him, What are these wounds in Thine hands? Then He shall answer, Those with which I was wounded in the house of My friends" (Zechariah 13:6).

OH, FATHER, *I'm completely blown away by Your love. It's so wide and deep and high. I'm also very sorry You have had to suffer so much on my account. I'm deeply ashamed of my insensitivity. Help me, dear Lord, to love like You do. Heal my jaded emotions. I want nothing more than to be faithful to You, my Friend, my Father, my Love. In Jesus. Amen.*

TWELVE

SIGHT FOR SORE EYES

Ultimately, our eternal survival is

that God's love

dependent on our knowing and believing

transcends our sin.

MY YOUNGEST DAUGHTER, Leah, and my son, Jason, were engaged one day in, shall we say, an *un*moving conversation. The topic? The meaning of the word *love*. After listening to Jason's explanation, little Leah told her older brother straight out, "You have no constipation of love."

Jason insisted, "I do, too, understand love, and it has nothing at all to do with *constipation*. Are you sure you don't mean *conception?*"

"No," Leah firmly replied, "I mean *constipation*. It means to understand something. If you don't believe me, you can look it up in the *dichotomy*."

Poor girl. She definitely was experiencing a dichotomy of sorts, but what she really needed was a dictionary. More often than not, Leah does know what she's talking about. I must admit, however, that on this occasion my precious little etymologist did need help.

Do you need help with your conception of love—God's love, specifically? If you were asked to write the entry on *love* for a new dictionary, how would it read?

The apostle Paul prayed that we would "comprehend" and "know" God's love. Then, in the next breath, he said that God's love "passeth knowledge" (Ephesians 3:18, 19), which means it cannot be understood by the mind alone, even if defined with correct words. To *know* the love of God is not merely an intellectual endeavor, such as studying mathematics or physiology. In order to be truly *comprehended* it must touch the inner person, captivating the emotions and the will, as well as the intellect. It must enter the realm of personal experience, moving past the territory of theoretical knowledge into the core of one's personhood, reshaping individual identity and purpose. This level of identification with God's love can only occur in one way. It must meet the most vital and basic need of our existence and become the solitary means of our very survival.

Allow me to explain what I mean. Weave together in your thinking the following three realities and the picture should become clear:

1. Sin is a destructive force and guilt is the means by which it destroys.

2. Our most basic and vital need for survival against that condemnation is to be embraced with a kind of love that refuses to condemn us even though we are rightfully condemnable. We need to be loved beyond any intrinsic deserving within ourselves, because, in fact, we do not deserve to be loved on the basis of our performance. This is not, however, because we are of no value. To the contrary! It is because our value in God's sight is far greater than can be measured by behavioral achievements or failures. When we see this kind of love, it liberates us from guilt and shifts our dependence from ourselves to the Source of that love.

3. This quality of love has only one Source. It has been fully manifested in One human being alone. In Jesus Christ, God has demonstrated His love toward us, not in mere words, but in the glorious reality of a life and death that has lavished grace upon us when we deserved condemnation. He loves us above and beyond our sin. Such is the nature of God's love.

The conclusion is self-evident. Ultimately, no human being will survive outside of knowing God's love on an experiential level. Apart from the healing power of this love, sin will slowly but surely crush the soul under its terrible weight, reaching the zenith of its destructive power in the final judgment. The great, inescapable reality of our guilt must be superseded in our perception by the far greater reality of God's unearnable mercy. Where sin abounds (and it abounds in our hearts), there God's grace *must* much more abound (see Romans 5:20). In our minds and emotions, the one dark reality must be swallowed up by the one enlightening reality. Every time our sin activates condemnation in our conscience, we must be able to agree with its claim and yet confidently point to the transcendent truth of divine love: "Yes, I am a sinner and my guilt is great. But God still loves me without reserve."

When God's love is understood on this level, it enters the interior realm of personal experience and becomes our vital dependence, our peace of mind, our joy of heart, our very will and reason to live.

Having stated this truth in my own words, let's now turn to Scripture for clarity and affirmation. There are at least three dimensions of divine love brought to view in the Bible.

1. *Selfless Love.* Jesus prayed just before His crucifixion, "O My Father, if it be possible, let this cup pass from Me: nevertheless not as I will, but as Thou wilt" (Matthew 26:39). Two wills are here in conflict—the *I will* and the *Thou wilt.* The sacrifice that lay before Christ aroused within Him the natural sense of self-preservation inherent in our humanity. He did not want to die. He did not want to endure the darkness of separation from His Father. But there was something He did not want even more. He did not want you and me to be eternally lost. Our life was a higher priority than His own. Therefore, He willingly submitted to the prospect of eternal death in order to give us eternal life.

When we say that God's love is *selfless,* we mean, in practical terms, that He loves without self-interest, but with a consuming other-centered interest. When God must choose between preserving Himself at the expense of others or preserving others at the expense of self, He always decides in favor of the others, even if the others are the very ones taking His life. There is no cutoff point to God's love, no stopping place beyond which He will not go. He holds nothing of Himself in reserve that will not be sacrificed for the good of others. His love reaches to the deepest possible level of self-sacrifice.

2. *Everlasting Love.* "I have loved thee with an everlasting love:

therefore with lovingkindness have I drawn thee" (Jeremiah 31:3). In this profound Scripture, the word *everlasting* is descriptive of the *kind* of love with which God loves us. To merely say, *I have loved you,* would leave the love undefined. God wants us to understand exactly what His love is like. So He says, *My love for you is everlasting.*

Everlasting love is love without end. Love that always *is* and never *is not.* Perpetual love. Unaffected love. Love that is not turned on or shut off by what we do or fail to do. It cannot be increased by our good performance or diminished by our bad performance. It simply, profoundly *is.* "God *is* love" (1 John 4:8). Always has been. Always will be. We can't earn it. We can't destroy it.

The everlasting facet of God's love naturally leads us into the next dimension.

3. *Non-Condemnatory Love.* John 3:16 is the most quoted of all Bible verses. Verse seventeen is just as vital. Take in the whole thought: "For God so loved the world, that He gave His only begotten Son, that whosoever believeth in Him should not perish, but have everlasting life. For God sent not His Son into the world to condemn the world; but that the world through Him might be saved" (John 3:16, 17).

Don't allow the significance of this incredible truth to escape your notice. You need it, as do I. Following the grammatical structure of the passage, we see that the *love* spoken of in verse sixteen is the antithesis of the *condemnation* mentioned in verse seventeen. In other words, God has defined His love by sending His Son to relate to us without condemnation. His love is, by nature, non-condemnatory. "For God so loved. . . that He gave His. . . Son. . .not. . .to condemn. . .but that the world through Him might be saved."

The condemnation we feel for sin arises out of the sin itself. Sin is wrong and our conscience knows it. We naturally and rightfully feel guilty for the sin we commit. Our guilt, in turn, weakens our will to do right by making us feel worthless and hopeless. The greater our guilt, the less value we see in ourselves. We interpret our failures as the true measure of our worth. Self-confidence is diminished. Self-respect is eroded. Moral strength is deflated. All we can do is give up to our sin.

There is only one possible solution for the sin problem. Hope is available in a single direction. We must see and believe that God's love transcends our guilt. This is the only remedy powerful enough to heal us. To know and trust that God loves us, in spite of our sin, will restore our sense of personal value and flood our souls with moral strength.

Stand with me for a moment on the outer edges of a crowd surrounding a man and a woman. Here we will witness divine love in action.

Do you see the woman? She has a bed sheet wrapped around her unclothed body. Cowering with fear, one of her hands is tightly hugged to her chest while the other covers her eyes, gesturing shame. Her long black hair hangs like stringy curtains around her tear-streaked face.

Now look at the crowd. They are mostly men, dressed in distinctively religious clothing. They are church leaders, the self-proclaimed representatives of God. These are the ones through whom the people think they see God.

Notice that one guy toward the front. Seems he is the main man among this lynch mob. His arms are crossed, one pushed up in front of his face with a bony index finger pointed at the woman. Contempt mingled with self-righteousness is written all over his countenance. What an ugly sight!

Then there's that singular figure, that other Man. The broken lady is forced before Him by her accusers. His hands are lifted slightly, at about waist level, partly opened, partly closed. His face reads like a paradox of conflicting emotions. As He looks at the mob, I see a grieving disappointment holding holy anger at bay. As He glances down at the woman, His eyes are flooded with compassionate longing to restore.

Listen, they're speaking.

We caught this woman in the very act of adultery and dragged her here for your verdict. According to the law, she ought to be stoned to death. But what do you think we should do with her?

You're not any more righteous than she is, Jesus replied, *so if you condemn her, you're condemning yourselves. If she ought to be stoned, so should you.*

The stark truth of His point was so inescapable that they were "convicted by their own conscience" and "went out one by one. . .and Jesus was left alone, and the woman standing in the midst" (John 8:9).

Then came an astonishing contradiction to popular religious opinion about how God thinks and feels toward lost, sinning sinners. I say *sinning sinners* because that's what this woman was. Not a repentant sinner—not yet. Not a confessing sinner—not yet. Not a reformed sinner—not yet. But a sinner caught in the very act. A sinner in sin and not yet out of it.

So how does God think, how does He feel toward us while we are yet sinners, before we stop sinning? Before we do right? Before we're even sorry?

Listen to Jesus:

"Woman, where are those thine accusers? Hath no man condemned thee? She said, No man, Lord. And Jesus said unto her, Neither do I condemn thee: go, and sin no more" (John 8:10, 11).

Incredible!

No condemnation.

He didn't say, "Repent of your sins and then I'll cease to condemn you." He said first, *I do not condemn you.* Then He said, in the light of His guilt-lifting love, *Go and sin no more.* The power to overcome the ongoing commission of sin is inherent in God's unearnable, non-condemnatory love. Condemnation perpetuates sin in the life. God's love, because it does not condemn, liberates the soul from sin.

Look at her now. . .after He has shown His love. Look beyond her face, behind her eyes, to the inner workings of her heart.

She lifts her head in response to His unique, astounding words. Prior to this she could imagine nothing but more of the same. More scorn. More rebuke. More condemnation. But He has painted a picture of God unlike any she has ever seen.

Sir, did I hear you right? Did you say you have no condemnation for me? Perhaps you don't understand. I am guilty.

Yes, I know. And yes, you did hear Me right. I said, I don't condemn you for your sin. I know you did it. I know you've done it over and over again. But I still don't feel any condemnation for you. I love you.

For the first time in her life Mary's eyes were resting upon the countenance of God. Those eyes, sore with the pain of a thousand condemning glares, including the self-hating glare in the mirror. Those eyes, sore with searching desire to see the true love of God. Those eyes were riveted upon the One who could rightly condemn, and He would not.

The beauty of His heart reached into hers and made it new. Adoration began to surge up from deep inside her abused soul.

Gratitude. Faith. Hope.

Oh, the sweet taste of hope.

Praise. Affection. Desire.

Desire to be whatever such a Savior would want her to be.

Strength. Resolve. Motivation.

Motivation to walk away from sin and live only for Him.

If I were asked to write a definition of God's love for a dictionary, it would read something like this:

1. The most beautiful thing in all the universe.

2. i.e., Jesus.

FATHER, *is that really You in Jesus? Do You really love me like He loved the woman caught in the act of adultery? I believe it is You, and I am amazed. I hardly know what to say. I love You so much. Thank You for loving me first. Hold on to me. Sometimes all I can hold on to is Your hold on me. Only in Jesus I pray. Amen.*

THIRTEEN
YOUR REFLECTION IN HIS EYES

At first she felt like a rich prostitute.

never was a

Eventually she felt like she

prostitute at all.

WHO ARE YOU? Yes, you, the one holding this book.

Jessica Monroe.

I don't mean your name. I'm not asking for the collection of alphabetical letters that compose the word by which you are called. Rather, I'm probing for your identity as a person.

I know what you're about to say.

I'm a human being of the female category, of Irish descent, a citizen of the United States of America, residing in California. I have a dad named Jim and a mom named Kathy and a dog named Bruno.

God knows all of that and every other detail of your involved and complicated life. But He also knows something else about you. . .a vital something else that you may or may not have discovered as of yet. But before we go there, let's continue a little further with who you are in your own estimation.

What did you say your name was? Oh, yes, Jessica.

Well, Jessica, have you ever stopped to reason backward in your family tree? Your parents had parents, who also had parents, who had parents as well. The weeping willow goes way back, in fact. All the way back to Adam and Eve, the original father and mother of all human beings. It was a glorious beginning. But it turned out to be a tragic start as well. Glorious because we were created, in our first parents, in the perfect image of God. Tragic because they blew it. But not only did they blow it for themselves, but for all of their posterity, you and me included. Because they became sinners, we're all sinners.

A major change of identity occurred in Adam and Eve for the

entire human race. By believing Satan's lies about their Father Creator, they shifted their allegiance to the deceiver and renounced their identity as children of God. Then the fallen couple proceeded to procreate in their own image, which was all they could do. They could only pass on what they themselves had, what they were.

So here we are. Sons and daughters of Adam and Eve. Sinners by inheritance, emotional depositories of a false picture of God by birth. We are sinfully ugly from day one. And your cute baby pictures have nothing to do with it. Looks can be deceiving. You were born a rebellious renegade, which, according to your parents, became apparent by the time you were two.

What a deal!

What a heritage!

What an identity!

And there's only one way out.

You need a complete identity change, as do I. A new Father. A new family. A new address. Even a new name. New ideas. New desires. All arising out of an entirely new picture of God, *the true picture.*

I heard a story once (in my imagination) of a red light district woman. She was raised in the party life of upper class prostitution. Her mother was a hooker as well, from the age of twenty. The woman despised her life, but it was all she knew. Her smile was plastic, because she never had a real one arise from within. Her face was painted with dark and light contrasting colors to try to give the appearance of a beauty she couldn't see in herself. On late mornings she would often cry tears of self-hatred wishing she were someone else, in another time and another place.

Then one day something totally strange and wonderful happened. She met a man who offered her more than her normal price.

"How much do you charge?" the man inquired.

When she named her fee, he smiled and said, "Too cheap. You're worth more than that."

"OK, mister," she responded, "How about we double the amount?"

"Still too little. You are worth far more than that."

The upward dickering continued until money was no object. She wondered if this guy was so rich that he had money to burn or if he was simply playing games with her head.

She could sense that he was dead serious.

"Why don't you take me on a world tour with no spending limit and give me a million dollars cash when it's all over?"

"No," he responded with a look of restrained emotion in his eyes. "You are far more valuable than that."

"Who are you, mister, the richest man in the world?"

"Perhaps, perhaps not, but I know value when I see it, and you are extremely valuable—worth all I have."

"So what do you want from me?"

"Just one thing. I'll give you all that I have. You'll never want for anything again. I'll supply all your needs. I only ask for one thing in exchange. Never again sell yourself to any man. Treat yourself like an innocent woman who has never turned a trick."

"What! Don't you see what I am? I'm a prostitute."

"Yes, I see what you are. But I don't see a prostitute. I see a precious woman. A lovely lady. A beautiful person trapped in a life you really don't want to live. So I'm offering you a whole different life. A way out. A totally new identity."

You could say the man was just plain stupid, or you could say he was very intelligent, intelligent enough to see beyond predicament to potential.

You could call what he did pretending, or you could call it prophecy, a self-fulfilling prophecy poised for fulfillment if she would only believe.

You could call his view of the woman blindness, or you could call it faith, a hope-imparting faith that might give her a whole new identity to live up to, his faith in her arousing her faith in him.

I'm happy to tell you that this particular prostitute did accept the new identity offered her. (It's my story. I can do whatever I want with it.) At first she felt like merely a rich prostitute. But after a while she began to feel like the daughter of an extremely kind man. Eventually she felt like she never was a prostitute at all. The old person she once was became merely a distant memory she could no longer identify with. The gracious faith of the rich man transformed the sinful woman into what he desired her to be.

Now let's return to your identity and mine. I ask again, *Who are you? Who am I? Are we guilty sons and daughters of fallen Adam and Eve?*

Yes, that is a very real dimension of our reality, and if we choose to do so we can maintain that identity by continuing to identify with it.

But there is another reality awaiting our consideration, just as real but even more powerful. There is a sense in which all that is true of us through Adam is not true of us at all, if we will but choose, instead, the identity God has chosen for us and given to us in Christ.

"For if by one man's offence death reigned by one; much more they which receive abundance of grace and of the gift of righteousness shall reign in life by One, Jesus Christ. Therefore as by the offence of one judgment came upon all men to condemnation; even so by the righteousness of One the free gift came upon all men unto justification of life. For as by one man's disobedience many were made sinners, so by the obedience of One shall many be made righteous" (Romans 5:17-19).

In Jesus Christ, God has created for us an entirely new identity and destiny. We need not continue to be who we are by natural birth, but may become sons and daughters of God by spiritual birth into the life of Christ. All we need to do is believe what He believes about us, see ourselves as He sees us, reckon ourselves by faith to be all He wants us to be. Adam sinned and brought condemnation "upon all men." His single failure created a universal sin problem that has impacted all of us. But Christ corrected that failure by living a sinless life in the very same humanity Adam passed down. His life of righteousness created a universal righteousness that all may tap into as a free gift.

Because of the perfect righteousness that is an achieved reality in Christ, God has faith in our potential by His grace. (His faith is so strong that He "calleth those things which be not as though they were" (Romans 4:17). In Paul's context he means that God regards us as righteous, not sinful, even though we are sinful and not righteous. By so doing He does not intend to excuse or perpetuate our sin, but rather to give us, as a gift, an entirely new identity of innocence and righteousness. He knows that to condemn us as the spiritual prostitutes we are would only harden us in our sin and perpetuate the moral weakness our guilt imposes. So He lifts the guilt in order to place our feet on vantage ground. By relating to us as beautiful, while we are yet ugly, He hopes to arouse in us a true desire for beauty. By regarding us as righteous, while we are yet sinners, He intends to ignite in us the confidence and hope needful to actually attain righteousness. So He "calls things that are not as though they were" (NIV).

Our part is to respond with like faith. We must see ourselves as He does. "Reckon yourselves to be dead indeed to sin, but alive to God in Christ Jesus our Lord" (Romans 6:11, NKJV). To reckon means to regard, to consider, to believe ourselves to be what we are not, that we may, by thus identifying ourselves, truly become what He wants us to be.

A physician does not become a physician by merely learning from books what a physician is. After all the book-learning, he still is not truly a physician. But he must regard himself to be what he is not in order to become what he wants to be. He must *practice* medicine as one who has never practiced medicine in order to be a medical doctor.

Likewise, we are not righteous. But God relates to us as righteous in order to instill in us the needed confidence to practice righteousness. "Therefore do not let sin reign in your mortal body, that you should obey it in its lusts. And do not present your members as instruments of unrighteousness to sin, but present yourselves to God as being alive from the dead, and your members as instruments of righteousness to God. For sin shall not have dominion over you, for you are not under the law but under grace" (Romans 6:12-14, NKJV).

In other words, live like who you are in Christ, not like who you are in yourself through Adam. This is possible because you are not under the condemnation of the law as a transgressor, but under the grace of God by which He reckons you as righteous through the faith of Jesus.

You may look at your life and see defeat, but in Christ you are more than a conqueror (see Romans 8:37).

You may feel abandoned, but in Christ you are an adopted child of God (see Ephesians 1:5).

You may feel rejected and condemned for your sins, but you are "accepted in the Beloved," Christ Jesus (see Ephesians 1:6).

You are all of this and infinitely more, because He was all of this for you in the very same humanity you are. In that humanity, your humanity and mine, He "consecrated for us" "a new and living way" (Hebrews 10:20). He forged out an entirely new humanity of our old humanity. Entering into our very situation of weakness and defeat, He "condemned sin in the flesh" (Romans 8:3) by refusing to yield to its power. He did this, not to pretend that we are something we are not, not to justify our sin, but to give us a new beginning point, so "that the righteousness of the law might be fulfilled in us, who walk not after the flesh, but after the Spirit" (Romans 8:4).

You could call Him foolish for regarding us as righteous before we actually are, or you could call Him extremely wise, wise enough to see beyond our predicament to our potential.

You could call what He has done mere pretending, or you could call it prophecy, a self-fulfilling prophecy poised for realization in all who believe.

You could call Him blind, or you could understand that His faith has given us an entirely new identity to live up to.

At first you'll feel like a wealthy wretch. But soon you'll begin to feel like the child of an extremely kind heavenly Father. Eventually the old person that you once were will become merely a distant memory you no longer identify with. The gracious faith of the rich Man, rich in righteousness and love, will transform you into the beautiful new person He has created in our humanity, in Christ.

So who are you, Jessica, or whatever your name may be? He has chosen you. Now the choice is yours.

MY FATHER: *Is it really so? Am I already all You want me to be in Christ? Was His humanity really my very humanity? Am I truly righteous in advance through faith in Jesus? I believe. Help Thou mine unbelief. Strengthen my faith in You to meet Your faith in me. May I never abuse Your amazing grace. Beautify me with the character of the One who embraced me before I even knew I needed Him. I love You, in the light of Your love for me. Hiding in Jesus, that He might be made manifest in me. Amen.*

FOURTEEN
THE LIE THAT BLINDS

Either God saves us because we're

He's good, then salvation is

good or because He's good. If because

ours *before* we're good.

AT ONE TIME I THOUGHT there were many different religions in the world. I could see lots of options: Buddhism. Hinduism. Islam. Judaism. Catholicism. Protestantism. Adventism. Mormonism. And a whole lot of other isms. After some thought and investigation, I'm now convinced that there are really only two religions to choose between. On the one hand, there are various renditions of one false religion. On the other hand, in contrast, there is one true religion, one truth about God.

The one false religion clothes itself in many different theological suits, to suit the 31 flavors taste of the human heart. Some are strong and blatant. Others are subtle and sweet. But when stripped naked, they're all the same. Many expressions of one basic concept. Many frames, but one very identical picture of God.

The one true religion is what it is and it's very clear about what it is. No subtle nuances. Just plain-Jane reality in all its unmistakable beauty.

So how can we know the difference?

The whole question hinges on one crucial factor alone: that which makes a religion true or false is its view of how God saves people. With regards to salvation, there are only two possibilities, which arise out of two conflicting views of God's character.

Option one: the foundation of every false religion is precisely the same, making them all one. That foundation is salvation by works. In this view, God is the offended party. He is in need of appeasement, for there is enmity in His heart toward the sinner. His finger is pointed in condemnation and His brow is furrowed in anger as He demands obedience and threatens to punish those who fail to measure up. "Turn or burn," is His motto. "Get your act together or I'll tear you apart."

The onus of responsibility to mend the relationship rests upon fallen man. He must do something to win, earn or merit God's disenchanted favor. He must do something—whatever the given religion might deem that something to be—to change God's posture toward him. Self-denial. Penance. Prayers. Pilgrimages. Payments of money. Fasting. Self-inflicted suffering. Divinely-inflicted suffering. Confessions. Dietary rules. Celibacy. Ceremonies. Sacrifices. Sabbath observance.

Doesn't matter what the something is, whether a man-made rule or a God-given command, the idea is the same. We humans need to do something to change God. Our goodness prompts His. God saves people in exchange for their being good, not because He is good. Our self-generated achievements arouse in God a change of heart. Whereas once He rejected us, now that we've done right, He accepts us. Whereas once He was hostile, now He is willing to forgive. He sings background harmony to our rather impressive song about our religious experience.

Problem is, our experience is not always so impressive. So in the face of our failures, the salvation-by-works picture of God forces us into despair or dishonesty. We either give up and turn from God altogether, or we give in to the temptation to rationalize our sin and imagine ourselves to be righteous. Self-hatred or self-righteousness are the only inevitable alternatives for the person who believes that God saves on the basis of good behavior.

Option two: the only true religion is embodied and personified in Jesus Christ. In Him we encounter a picture of God that is the complete antithesis of the salvation-by-works view. In the life and death of Jesus we see a God who saves wholly by His grace, by the sheer unprompted, unearned, intrinsic goodness of His own character. Human beings tap into that salvation by faith; that is, by believing the picture of God revealed in Christ.

In this view, man is the offended party. There is "enmity" in his heart toward God (see Romans 8:7) due to Satan's misrepresentation of the divine character. Evading the truth of his own guilt, man's accusing finger is pointed heavenward as he rebels against his Maker.

The sinner's only hope is for God to take responsibility, to take blame, to take painful effort to prove His love and win back our trust. God must do something—something amazing, awesome, awful—to demonstrate the truth of His goodness. He must do something to change our hearts toward Him.

And so He does.

Jesus, "though He was in the form of God, did not count equality with God something to be grasped, but emptied Himself, taking the form of a servant, being born in the likeness of men. And being found in human form He humbled Himself and became obedient unto death, even the death of the cross" (Philippians 2:6-8, RSV).

Incarnation. Condescension. Self-denial. Humiliation. Giving to the takers. Loving the unlovable. Forgiving the unforgiving. Caring for the uncaring. Giving all in exchange for nothing, and thereby creating in us the capacity to give.

What God does transforms us. His self-generated achievements in Christ arouse in us a change of heart. He moves toward us of His own initiative, unprompted by our good deeds and undetoured by our sinfulness. In fact, our condition draws Him rather than repels Him. He runs to meet our need. He saves us because He is good, not in exchange for our goodness. And then, in turn, His goodness leads us to repent of our sins (see Romans 2:4). His unmerited love arouses in our hearts an obedient love for Him. "We love Him because He first loved us" (1 John 4:19).

His love is primary, original, unborrowed.

Ours is secondary, derived, responsive.

His love is creative.

Ours is created.

His love and goodness makes ours possible.

His beautiful character will beautify ours as we behold Christ.

Whereas once we rejected Him, now that we see His love for us in Christ, we embrace Him as all our hearts ever really needed. Whereas once we were hostile toward Him, now we are soft and moldable in His trustworthy hands. We sing background harmony to the impressive song of His amazing love. And His love is so impressive, in fact, that it empowers us to walk away from our sin, shaking our heads in astonishment that we could have ever been so blind. But we were. We were blinded by the lie that God saves the good. Blinded by the lie that we can actually do good before He saves us. Blinded by the lie that the good we do gains something from Him that He has not already lavished upon us as a free gift in Christ.

Somebody holding this book is getting nervous. I feel the book shaking. You know who you are. You're worried that a completely free salvation would give license to sin and make obedience to God's law unnecessary. *We can't have God saving sinners one hundred percent by grace,* you're thinking, *because then there wouldn't be any reason to live a godly life. We could live any way we please and still be saved.*

Allow me to explain why the opposite is true.

The salvation-by-works picture of God does produce an illusionary appearance of obedience to God, but never the real thing. It arouses an outward compliance with the letter of the law, but leaves the heart unchanged. This is because the salvation-by-works picture drives the sinner with a sense of responsibility to win God's favor, but does not draw the sinner with a sense of God's goodness. Therefore, the root-structure of the sin problem, which is self-centeredness, remains unresolved. Fear of personal loss and desire for personal gain prompt a mere obligatory obedience to a God whom we still do not truly love. He is yet undesirable in our eyes, but we do what we've got to do in order to escape hell and gain heaven. Which means, actually, that we're not serving Him at all, but rather ourselves. And that leaves us right where we started—as unsaved, self-serving rebels. Only difference is, now we go to church and think we're God's faithful people.

The moment human deeds of any kind are placed ahead of salvation as a prerequisite, the empowering potential of the gospel is robbed, the essence of divine love is hidden from view, and fallen man is exalted above God in character. He is made out to be our dependent rather than we His. He is expected to change in response to our goodness, rather than we in response to His, which makes Him the smaller person and us the bigger. This is precisely why the salvation-by-works picture of God is so popular—because it nourishes our natural urge for self-exaltation. We began our rebellion with a desire to live independent of God and exalt ourselves to a plane of equality with Him. It is logical, then, that every religion we humans come up with will continue to foster that quest for self-exaltation.

The salvation-by-grace picture of God, unlike the salvation-by-works view, does, in fact, liberate from sin and produce genuine obedience to God's holy law; not sometimes, but always, if it is truly believed. The truth never fails to set the believer free (see John 8:32). It does this by changing the heart, which, in turn, changes the life as well. The true revelation of the divine character awakens in the mind and emotions a deep, cleansing sense of self-abandoning love for such an incredible God. Once aroused in the soul, this love unavoidably leads the sinner into a life of loyal, affectionate submission to God's will. All human glory is laid in the dust, opening the way for God to do for us what we cannot do for ourselves.

The Bible declares only one way of salvation:

"By grace [God's unearnable love] are ye saved [liberated from the guilt and power of sin] through faith [by believing and receiving Christ as the truth about God]; and that not of yourselves: it is the gift of God [absolutely free]: not of [earned by] works, lest any man should boast [of having any meritorious part in his salvation]. For [because] we are His workmanship [His masterpiece], created [not self-generated] in Christ Jesus unto good works [which are the product of our salvation not its means of attainment], which God hath before [our involvement] ordained [achieved in Christ] that we should walk in them" (Ephesians 2:8-10).

There is no danger at all of making God's goodness too good. The real danger is in failing to even come close to its surpassing greatness. Without question, there will always be those "who change the grace of our God into a license for immorality" (Jude 4, NIV). So be it. But God is who He is. If we choose to rebel against Him in the light of His kindness, then His grace is not to be blamed. For the ones who truly believe, that same grace, so far from an excuse for sin, moves them to "say 'no' to ungodliness and worldly passions, and to live self-controlled, upright and godly lives in this present age" (Titus 2:11, 12, NIV).

FATHER: *I can see that Satan is multifarious in his deceptions, but at foundation level he has but one lethal lie: Your favor, he would have us believe, must be earned by right doing on our part. With such an insurmountable obstacle before them, many will never even try to approach You. Others will zealously pour themselves into self-righteousness and remain blind to Your love. Still others will simply cast off such an ugly notion of Deity and deny Your existence altogether. Thank You for opening my eyes to Your unearnable grace. May I never abuse it as an excuse for sin. May Your goodness awaken within me an unstoppable quest to honor You in every aspect of my life. In Christ Jesus I pray. Amen.*

FIFTEEN

BECAUSE WE'RE FREE, WE NEED TO SEE

Communication = understanding.

Love = Loyalty. At this point

more, nor anything less,

than friendship acted out.

Understanding = trust. Trust = love.

obedience is nothing

IF I WERE TO HOLD A GUN to your head and say *jump*, you'd jump. If I said *smile*, you'd smile. If I said *stand on your head*, you'd try.

Behavior can be controlled with force.

But what if I held a gun to your head and said, *love me. . . feel affectionate toward me. . .trust me?*

Could you?

I didn't ask *would you*, as if it would be a simple matter of choice. I asked, *could you?* Would it even be within the realm of possibility for you to love and trust me with a gun in my hand pointed at your head? (I do not here speak of the kind of love we are to have for even our enemies, but of the trusting kind of love that is accompanied by loyalty and devotion.)

Of course not. You may lie to me with your mouth to save your life, but in your heart you simply could not really love and trust me. Feelings of love and trust are mutually exclusive from force and manipulation. They cannot coexist in the same conscious reality of any human experience. If love is to occur at all, it must occur among circumstances in which you are free to love or not to love. If trust is to be established in your heart for any person, it can only happen if you truly see that person as trustworthy.

Because we are free, we need to see. Especially is this true with regards to our relationship with God.

This is why the inspired songwriter sang to the Lord, "Give me understanding, and I shall keep Your law; indeed, I shall observe it with my whole heart" (Psalm 119:34, NKJV).

The Bible here links *understanding* with the movement of the *will* or *the power of choice*. Out of understanding comes *whole-heart* obedience to the Lord. If we were to obey God's law without understanding His character, our obedience would not be obedience at all, but rather slavery. I'm not suggesting that we are to have a stubborn attitude that requires perfect understanding before we will obey the Lord. Not at all. In fact, we will never perfectly comprehend the character and will of Almighty God. Faith will often require that we move in sync with His will even though we do not totally grasp all the whys and hows.

However...

It is vital that we come to understand the character of God to the degree that sincere love and trust are alive in the soul. Perfect perception is not a prerequisite to loyalty. On the other hand, to see God's law as arbitrary and His character as potentially cruel, and within that clouded perception to attempt obedience, would, indeed, equate to bondage. While we will never fully know the enormous depth of God's character and purposes, we must see Him clearly enough to believe He is completely good and, therefore, completely trustworthy.

Because God made us free moral beings with the power to choose whether or not we want to serve Him, He also made us with the intellectual and emotional capacity to understand and judge His worthiness. The more clearly we see God's character, the more free we will become to obey Him with *the whole heart*.

Please don't allow all this to sound haughty or bold, to suggest that mere human beings are to evaluate God's character. The Lord Himself would not have it any other way. He is the One who has created this type of arrangement between Himself and us. He is the One who made us with the freedom to choose. He also made us with the power to reason as the complementary component to that freedom. As far as I can see, the whole thing makes Him larger, not smaller. To think that He who is the sovereign God of the universe would choose to submit Himself to my evaluation persuades me all the more that He is completely transparent and trustworthy. If He demanded that I obey Him without any questions, and without any quest to know Him intimately, then I would doubt His integrity. But He has nothing to hide, nothing of which He is ashamed. There is nothing He fears I might discover that would turn me from Him. To the contrary, He is totally confident that the more I know of Him, the more I will love and trust Him. He is infinitely worthy of my deepest loyalty and highest reverence, and He knows it. He knows it, not as a matter of divine conceit, but because He knows the intrinsic goodness of the principles by which He operates. He knows He loves us and always acts in our best interest. "For I know the thoughts that I think toward you, says the Lord, thoughts of peace and not of evil, to give you a future and a hope" (Jeremiah 29:11, NKJV).

How fitting, then, that Jesus would come to earth as God's representative and invite us into enlightened friendship rather than command us into blind slavery:

"No longer do I call you slaves; for the slave does not know what his master is doing; but I have called you friends, for all things that I have heard from My Father I have made known to you" (John 15:15, NASB).

The significance of this Scripture cannot be overstated. It communicates the essence of all God wants from human beings. He is aiming for the simple-deep intimacy of friendship. In order to illustrate just what He means, Jesus draws a contrast between two kinds of relationships with which we are very familiar: slavery versus friendship. Slavery is characterized by fear-motivated obedience. The slave does what he is told by his master simply because he is told, no questions asked, or else. Friendship, in distinct contrast, is characterized by a love-motivated loyalty. A person does what his friend asks because he wants to, not because he had better. Friends are compelled by an inner sense of loyalty and a desire to please.

According to Jesus, our friendship with Him is born out of communication, which brings us back to our need for understanding. Did you notice what He said: "I have called you friends, for [because] all things [information] that I have heard from My Father I have made known to you [communication]."

Out of communication comes understanding.
Out of understanding comes trust.
Out of trust comes love.
Out of love comes loyalty.

At this point obedience is not really an issue. In friendship with God, obedience is not a hassle or a burden or even a question. To the extreme contrary, it is the deepest passion and highest quest of the heart. Obedience is the natural offspring of trust-motivated love. King David had this kind of obedience in mind when he sang, "I *delight* to do Thy will, O my God: yea, Thy law is within my *heart*" (Psalm 40:8). This is what the apostle Paul had in mind when he said, "Obey. . .obey. . . . But God be thanked that. . .ye have obeyed from the heart" (Romans 6:16, 17). All true obedience arises out of the *heart* and is attended by a deep inner sense of personal *delight*. You could call it obedience, or you could call it friendship. They are one and the same.

Fear-motivated obedience is not obedience at all. It's like the little boy who stood up in class to ask a question. When the teacher ordered him to sit down, he refused. So the teacher shoved the persistent little guy into his seat, snarling, "I said, *Sit down*." The boy replied, "I'm sitting down with my body, but I am standing up in my mind." As someone once said, "A man convinced against his will is of the same opinion still."

To comply with the letter of God's law out of a mere sense of obligation, merely because we feel fearful of doing otherwise, is not really obedience. It is rebellion in disguise. Love is the Lord's higher aim. As love increases in the soul, fear diminishes. "There is no fear in love; but perfect love casteth out fear: because fear hath torment. He that feareth is not made perfect in love. We love Him because He first loved us" (1 John 4:18, 19). We come to the place where we love God without fear as we comprehend His love for us. His love for us precedes our love for Him and makes it possible for us to love Him. When we see His love for us, that very seeing gives birth to love in our hearts for Him. Love awakens love and chases fear away.

Under the inspiration of the Holy Spirit, Zacharias prayed

that God would "grant unto us that we…might serve Him [God] *without fear*, in holiness and righteousness" (Luke 1:74, 75). Paul expressed similar thoughts as he described the Christian's relationship with God: "Ye have not received the spirit [disposition] of bondage again to fear; but ye have received the Spirit of adoption, whereby we cry, Abba, Father" (Romans 8:15).

It is God's desire that we would "serve Him without fear," that we would not be in bondage to fear as we relate to Him. Rather, He longs for us to perceive Him as a loving, gracious Father of whom we need not be afraid. And we need not be afraid of Him for a good reason: He is not scary.

God is not ugly, but beautiful.

He is not mean, but kind.

Not condemnatory, but forgiving.

Not arbitrary, but consistent.

Not moody, but predictable.

Not evil, or even a combination of good and evil, but one hundred percent good all the time.

The problem is not with who God is, but with who we think He is. Fear arises out of misconceptions of His character. On the other hand, fear subsides and love arises as we see His character in its true light. The Bible is filled with promises that persuade us of the power inherent in an understanding of God's character. Consider just a few:

Paul prayed that "the Father of glory may give unto you the spirit [disposition] of wisdom and revelation in the knowledge of Him: the eyes of your understanding being enlightened" (Ephesians 1:17, 18). That you "may be able to comprehend …and to know the love of Christ, which passeth knowledge, that ye might be filled with all the fullness of God" (Ephesians 3:18, 19).

Peter recognized that "grace and peace" enter the life through "the knowledge of God, and of Jesus our Lord, according as His divine power hath given unto us all things that pertain unto life and godliness, through the knowledge of Him" (2 Peter 1:2, 3).

John explained that "the love of God was manifested toward us" in that He "sent His only begotten Son into the world, that we might live through Him" (1 John 4:9, NKJV). We are to "*behold* what manner [what kind, what quality, what depth] of love the Father hath bestowed upon us" (1 John 3:1).

Jesus Himself said, "This is life eternal, that they might know Thee the only true God, and Jesus Christ, whom Thou hast sent" (John 17:3).

Because God has made us free, He has also made us with the need to see clearly enough to make intelligent decisions. He is eager to enlighten all who want to know Him. He will never put a gun to your head. He's not a control freak. He's an intimate Friend.

YOU ARE SO VERY WONDERFUL, LORD. *To think that the Sovereign Ruler of the universe desires friendship with me! The thought is too high for me to comprehend. But I believe it, because I see the proof in Christ. He has made the longing of Your heart absolutely clear. He has opened the way for me to know and love You without fear. Yes, with awesome reverence, for You are Almighty God, but without frightful fear. I am won. You are my all in all. Hold on to me tight until I reach the other side. In the light of Christ's character, I pray. Amen.*

SIXTEEN

WHAT YOU SEE
IS WHAT YOU GET

The single most **vital** issue we will ever

hearts of the

deal with is the picture we hold in our

character of God.

I COULD SENSE that the military-looking man wanted to tell me something. But he was hesitant. Every few minutes he would move to the front of his seat and lean forward as if he were going to speak, only to sit back again. To this point I had done most of the talking, a friendly visit about the trivia of life.

Finally, I could take the suspense no longer. As the temptation rose within me to slap the back of his head (which is on the opposite side of the mouth) in an effort to get the words out, I figured I had better break the ice for him and spare myself the embarrassment of the other method.

"Excuse me, Tommy, but is there something you would like to share with me? Maybe I'm misreading you, but if there is something on your heart, please feel free to open up."

"Yes," he smiled with a visible sense of relief, "there is something I'd like to share—my personal testimony of God's leading in my life. Would you mind?"

I responded eagerly to the offer. Tommy had just heard my testimony in a seminar I was conducting at a church near his home. Now he wanted to tell the story of his own journey to the heavenly Father through a rather unique encounter with his earthly father.

Tommy began. . .

I grew up never knowing my father. And yet I did have a picture of him in my mind, thanks to my mother.

There were two things she told me over and over again as I grew up. *You're a selfish, worthless little monster of a child.* And then she'd always add, *You're just like your father.*

It seemed to me that the more these thoughts lodged in my mind, the more helpless I felt to be well-behaved. I became more and more like my dad, like the dad I saw in my imagination, and I hated him.

On a few occasions I asked my mom about Dad. She was quick to inform me that he wasn't worth knowing. *If he loved you,* she would say, *don't you think he'd call sometime or at least send a birthday card once a year?*

As I grew into manhood, life became harder and harder. The military was my escape. For a while the rigor and discipline seemed to channel my frustration. But I could never fully evade the fact that I was an ugly person inside. I hated myself and nearly everyone around me. Then something happened that changed everything.

Mom made a shocking announcement to family and friends. For years she had been living a secret lesbian lifestyle. Now she wanted to have the freedom to do so openly without any hassles. For some reason, this startling news awakened in me a desire to meet my father for myself. I wondered if all Mom had told me was true. By asking around among the family, I came up with the name of a town four states away from where I lived. Directory assistance supplied me with a possible phone number.

My hand trembled as I punched the buttons on my phone.

McGregor here, the voice answered abruptly on the other end.

Dad, I spoke, *I mean Mr. McGregor, this is Tommy, your son. Please don't hang up. I don't know if you want anything to do with me, and I don't mean to trouble you, but I'm an adult now. I have a wife and three children. If at all possible, I would really like to meet you, at least one time.*

As my stomach turned with fear of rejection, a soft and eager voice replied, *I'd be pleased to meet you, son.*

I proceeded to make travel arrangements. The plane ticket was purchased, a rental car reserved. Finally, after years of bitterness, hatred and confusion, the day of first-hand encounter arrived. I stood in front of an old farmhouse. A tractor was propped up on a tree stump, obviously undergoing repairs. There were evidences of long years of labor everywhere around the small home. Again my whole insides churned as I stood there on the creaky wooden porch.

An old man opened the door, slightly hunched over from years of hard work on the farm. His eyes seemed nervous, but gentle.

Mr. McGregor, I'm Tommy.

Please come in, son. His voice was as gentle as his eyes.

We sat across from each other on separate chairs. It was obvious that neither of us knew what to say. After a few seconds of silence, we both slowly stood up and extended our hands. He pulled me to himself and embraced me. He was so different than I had imagined.

After shedding a few tears, I couldn't contain myself any longer. He seemed kind, but what about everything Mom had told me. I poured out my questions, demanding answers.

Why did you bring me into the world and then divorce Mom for another woman? Why were you so cruel to her? Why didn't you care about me? Why haven't I ever heard from you, not one call or even a letter in all these years?

The old farmer looked bewildered and grieved. Sitting down, he began to explain.

I've never loved any other woman but your mother. I still love her, although I haven't seen her for many years. There never was another woman. She just up and left one day. I've remained alone all these years, hoping that some day she would come back. I wish I could have called or written. Better yet, I would have visited. But I had no idea where she took you. After a few years passed by, I determined to never move from this farm, thinking that maybe someday you'd grow up and come find me.

I found out that my dad is a fine old hillbilly gentleman, the finest man I've ever known. When I discovered that my father was such a good guy, it changed me. All my bitterness and anger melted away in the realization of his love for me. A strange, effortless softening settled into my heart. It seemed as though all the conflicts of my life were resolved in that moment of truth when I met my father for myself and discovered that he was a man worth knowing and emulating. Prior to this point in my life I had always hated God and believed He was a cruel heavenly sadist who found pleasure in our pain. But somehow, meeting my dad opened me up to meeting my heavenly Father.

Tommy's mother had lied to him. Through her misrepresentation he grew up hating the father he never knew. But actually he didn't hate his dad; he hated a false image which had no basis in reality. Once he discovered the truth of his father's good character, his whole perspective on life was transformed.

There are lots of issues we humans have to deal with, lots of problems to solve and perplexities to unravel. But the most crucial issue any of us will ever grapple with is the picture we hold in our hearts of the character of God. The most significant matter we will ever ponder is the identity of Deity. The most vital problem we will ever endeavor to solve is the conflict in our heads between clashing images of the One in the heavens who is our Father.

Like Tommy, we've been lied to from the beginning. Our Father's character has been terribly misrepresented. Some of the bad rumors are blatantly slanderous, noised abroad by His avowed enemies. Others are subtle insinuations woven into the theology of those who claim to be His friends. There's only one way to know the truth: we must have a firsthand, personal encounter with the Father for ourselves.

Our perception of God's character is the fulcrum of our existence, the pivotal point upon which all the significant matters of life turn. Whether we are conscious of the fact or not, the way we see God plays a major role in shaping us into who we are. The picture of God we hold in our hearts sets up within us a psychological template, a pattern of thinking and feeling, which serves as the basic perceptual paradigm by which our conscience will see and judge others *and* self. The way we view God's character toward us strongly influences how we relate to everyone around us, and will ultimately determine how we relate to ourselves.

In the spiritual dimension of life, by beholding we are changed: "We all, with open face beholding as in a glass the glory [character] of the Lord, are changed into the same image" (2 Corinthians 3:18). "For as he [a man] thinketh in his heart, so is he" (Proverbs 23:7). If you see God as condemnatory when you fail, then you will tend to condemn and reject others when they fail. On the other hand, if you see in God a changeless love for your own soul, then you will love others even when they fail.

The final and inevitable step in this psychological process is either bitter or sweet, depending on your paradigm of God's character. Your perception of God's character toward you, which in turn shapes the way you relate to others, will eventually form in you the psychological boundaries by which you will finally be judged within your own conscience. The more deeply and consistently you see God as a condemnatory judge, the more you will relate to others with condemnation, and the less capable you will become of believing that God forgives you in your time of need. Forgiveness becomes off limits, not because God refuses to forgive, but because you cannot see Him as forgiving. The perceptual and emotional capacity to discern God's love is destroyed by persistently refusing to love others.

Jesus articulated the whole concept like this (pay close attention to His words as though you have never read them before):

"Love your enemies, do good to those who hate you, bless those who curse you, and pray for those who spitefully use you. . . . But if you love those who love you, what credit is that to you?

For even sinners love those who love them. And if you do good to those who do good to you, what credit is that to you? For even sinners do the same. . . . But love your enemies, do good, and lend, hoping for nothing in return; and your reward will be great, and you will be sons of the Most High. For He is kind to the unthankful and evil. Therefore be merciful, just as your Father also is merciful. Judge not, and you shall not be judged. Condemn not, and you shall not be condemned. Forgive, and you will be forgiven. Give, and it will be given to you. . . . For with the same measure that you use, it will be measured back to you" (Luke 6:27, 32, 33, 35-38, NKJV).

Follow the simple-deep logic of what Christ is saying here. He communicates three vital realities:

1. Jesus calls upon us to relate to unrepentant sinners as though they weren't sinners at all. We are to love, do good toward, pray for, bless, give to, forgive and refrain from condemning those who are evil and spiteful, while they are evil and spiteful, not after they have repented.

2. Then Jesus builds an incredible bridge of understanding from this admonition. The reason we are to relate to others in this way is because this is exactly how God relates to all sinners when they are His enemies, ourselves included. Before we repent, while we are in rebellion against Him, He loves us. He does good for us, blesses us, forgives us without condemnation. "Therefore," Jesus concludes, "be merciful, just as [in the same way] your Father also is merciful." To relate to the evil and thankless with love and mercy makes us children of the Most High, because by so doing we are thinking and feeling and acting as He does.

3. The final point made by the Savior is extremely serious. The same standard of measurement, He explains, which we use to judge others will be measured back to us. Obviously, Jesus does not mean that God will condemn us if we condemn others. He just made it clear that God does not operate within a system of condemnation. Never will the Creator's character change to reflect our ugliness back to us. God *is* forgiving. He does not condemn, even the unthankful and evil. He cannot cease to be

who and what and how He is. But Jesus wants us to understand that if we insist on a system of condemnation in our dealings with others, we are burning the bridge of forgiveness over which we ourselves must pass. We are backing ourselves into an inescapable corner of condemnation. Mercy is the only passageway out of our guilt, but we eliminate our ability to grasp that solitary rescue by refusing to pardon those who wrong us.

If you see condemnation in God, you'll give condemnation to others and finally experience condemnation upon yourself. But if you see the liberating forgiveness that is truly in the Lord, you'll give forgiveness to others and finally rest in the assurance of personal forgiveness. What you see is what you get. You are what you see and believe, and it will one day return to either haunt or bless.

Life's vital issue, then, is that we see our Father as He really is. When we do, we will discover that He is truly the finest Person in all the universe.

Thanks Tommy. . . and Mr. McGregor.

MY FATHER, *thank You for waiting so many years while I wandered anywhere but toward You. It is clear to me now that the god I saw and despised in my imagination wasn't You at all. Now that I've come to know You for myself, I see that You are truly the finest Person in all the universe. And in that revelation is the secret power of my transformation. By beholding the goodness of Your character, I am changed. In the light of Your pardoning love for me, I sense in my heart the melting away of all condemnation for others. Indeed, how can one forgiven rebel condemn another? And yet, while I know this truth, I am in extreme need of Your continual attention. Keep your beautiful face ever before me, that I revert not back to the hard, cold heart I have left behind. In the light of the character of Christ I pray. Amen.*

SEVENTEEN

FEEL WHAT YOU SEE

There is a lovely place in the human soul

God waits at that place.

where intellect and emotion intersect.

Have you ever been there?

WHEN I BEGAN COMPOSING thoughts for this book, I intended to end up with something different than what I now have. I guess it was my original goal to communicate complex theological truths in simple, realistic terms. It was a writing project, a task to undertake as a ministry to others. But each step of the way, with increasing awareness, I have sensed the ministering of the Lord to my own soul. A divine passion has gripped my heart with gradual intensity, nudging me into a spiritual realm beyond the reach of mere theological explanation.

While I still hope my initial purpose is achieved to a satisfying degree for you, the reader, I now hope for more. I hope that you also have been transported beyond words into a deeper experience with your Father. To merely grasp true ideas with the intellect is not, cannot be, the highest aim of our spiritual quest. We are more than mind; we are heart. We are feelers, not merely thinkers. To know God means nothing if we do not passionately love Him in the knowing.

There is a place in the human soul where intellect and emotion intersect, a region where mind and heart meet as one. It is here, at this intersection, that true Christianity occurs. It is here, where we feel with the heart what we understand with the mind, that deep and lasting transformation is attained. Truth is vital; but truth must be allowed to pass through the intellect and reach the inner spirit if it is to change us for the better.

Intellectual religion is often worn as a cloak to cover an underlying lack of real love-motivated commitment to a personal God. When caught in this snare, we tend to specialize in doctrinal debate and outward conformity to the letter of the law. We are only secure when we are right, for it is our intellectual correctness and our outward compliance that persuades us we are right with God. And yet, our rightness in precept and practice may be over-shadowed by a cold, albeit often cultured, condemnation of those whom we think are below our spiritual stratosphere.

According to Jesus, God is on the search for an entirely different kind of worshiper: "The true worshiper shall worship the Father in spirit and in truth: for the Father seeketh such to worship Him" (John 4:23).

These words were spoken to a woman who had sought the fulfillment of her heart in the "love" of six different men. Her life was one of failed romances, one after another, yielding an ever-enlarging, God-size hole in her soul. Jesus was the seventh man in her life, Mr. Right after all. He diagnosed her condition as one of heart-thirsting that could only be quenched by divine passion.

What you're looking for, Jesus seemed to say, *is the very thing God happens to be looking for; the two of you are a perfect match. He is searching for true worshipers, as you are searching for true love.*

God is longing for worshipers who put heart as well as head into the relationship; worshipers who feel as well as think. It is not by literary chance that the prophets of the Old Testament repeatedly portray God as a jilted lover longing for the attention of His unfaithful people (see Ezekiel 16). God is not mere cerebral energy. Like us, He is more than mind. He is heart. He is emotion. He is a feeler, not merely a thinker. "God is love."

To worship the Divine Romancer in truth alone is a slap in the face, not unlike a woman marrying a man because it is the most intelligent thing to do. After all, He is wealthy. Call it smart. Call it shrewd. Call it whatever you want. But don't call it love. Religion that is merely religion because it is right or true or intelligent, is something, but it is not worship, not the kind of worship God is searching for. The very idea that God—the Almighty Creator of all things—is seeking for anything at all is too much to grasp. But to think that what He desires is the heart-passion of rebels like you and me is nearly unbelievable. And it would be altogether unbelievable if He had not taken the convincing step of incarnating that desire in Christ to prove the depth of His affection for us.

Does God really long for love? Does the Almighty have a heart that feels as well as a mind that thinks?

Jesus says *Yes.*

Yes, God is actually on the scout for passionate lovers of His person. Lovers of His love, His kindness, His mercy, His justice. Lovers of His character. He is interested in a long-term relationship—eternity together in mutual love and trust. He is seeking true worshipers who worship Him in heart as well as in truth. Worshipers who feel what they see in Him.

"Deep is calling to deep." The depths of God's heart is calling out to the deepest part of your heart.

Do you hear Him; do you feel Him?

Will you answer?

HERE I AM LORD. *My mind for Your truth; my heart for Your love. Everything that I am I willingly give to You. No reserve, as if there could be anything in this world even slightly comparable to all I have in You. No fear, as if there were any question of Your goodwill toward me. No doubt, as if Your love were not clear enough in Christ. And yet, I sense that I am extremely weak. So please do not let go of me. . .I know You never will. I pray in the glorious light of Your character as it is revealed in Jesus. Amen.*

A sneak preview of Ty Gibson's
Shades of Grace: Exploring the depths of God's healing love
Pacific Press® Publishing Association, © 2001.

"God longs for us to feel after Him and find Him because He loves us with all the energy of His divine being. It is the nature of His love to continually reach out of Himself in tireless efforts to secure our eternal happiness, which is only possible as we embrace His love and allow it to flow freely out of our lives to Him and all others.

I still cry. In fact, I just shed tears yesterday. But now my tears are named.

They are tears of longing for more of God: 'As the deer pants for the water brooks, so pants my soul for You, O God. My soul thirsts for God, for the living God' (Psalm 42:1, 2, NKJV).

They are tears of joy for the pleasure of knowing His love: 'In Your Presence is fullness of joy; at Your right hand are pleasures forevermore' (Psalm 16:11, NKJV).

They are sometimes tears of sorrow for the times I ignore Him or misrepresent His beautiful character: 'Be merciful to me, O Lord, for I cry to You' (Psalm 86:3, NKJV).

I still cry. Do you?

Pause right now to identify your own tears. If they are yet nameless, recognize that your deepest heart-longings are for an intimate, eternal relationship with the divine Lover of your soul. If they are named, then I welcome you home to the heart of God."

Shades of Grace, by Ty Gibson, is available at your local ABC.

******

Other books by Ty Gibson:

Abandon Ship?
Is the organized SDA Church still God's recognized movement on earth? 0-8163-1364-4. Paperback. US$8.99, Cdn$13.99.

In the Light of God's Love
Personal salvation, obedience, temptation, failure, and relationships—all are pondered with fresh insight under the illuminating light of divine love. 0-8163-1334-2. Paper. US$9.99, Cdn$15.49.

Order from your ABC by calling **1-800-765-6955**, or get online and shop our virtual store at <u>**<www.adventistbookcenter.com>**</u>.

• Read a chapter from your favorite book
• Order online
• Sign up for email notices on new products